LIFE@WORK®

MARKETPLACE SUCCESS FOR PEOPLE OF FAITH

Published in Nashville, Tennessee, by Thomas Nelson, Inc.

Published in association with Yates & Yates, LLP, Attorneys and Counselors, Orange, California.

Library of Congress Cataloging-in-Publication Data

Maxwell, John C., 1947–
  Life@work : marketplace success for people of faith / John C. Maxwell, Stephen R. Graves, Thomas G. Addington.
     p. cm.
  Includes bibliographical references.
  ISBN 1-4002-8010-9
  1. Businesspeople—Religious life. 2. Business—Religious aspects—
Christianity. I. Graves, Stephen R., 1955– II. Addington, Thomas G. 1955–
III. Title.
 BV4596.B8M39 2005
  248.8'8—dc22   2005000104

Printed in the United States of America
1 2 3 4 5 6 QWK 08 07 06 05

Grant Nelson
Bill Townsend
Greg Spencer

Three men who refused to let Life@Work be just another empty turn of a phrase that sits on the shelf of never-developed ideas. Your resources launched Life@Work, and only the Lord knows the reach of your investment. Years later we are still staggered by your vision and energy to follow your heart.

Acknowledgments

David Scott
Andrew Brill

Thank you for redirecting your summer to researching, brainstorming, writing, and editing. Your ability to bring your calling and skill and wed them with serving and character was a daily exhibition of a Life@Work done right.

David, this was our first project with you, and I must say, you are as gifted a thinker in this space as we have come across in a long while. Eternal thanks and huge anticipation to see where the Lord takes you.

Thank you to the hundreds of men and women of faith who helped us shape the thinking of this book. Most of the stories used in this book have one of you in mind. While the stories are true, some details in some accounts have been changed to honor your privacy.

Contents

The Life@Work Test

Assess how sharp both edges of your Life@Work are by answering yes or no to the following statements:

- My skill set is sharper today than it was three years ago, and my boss would agree. _Yes _____ No _____

- My faith has made me "more valuable" to my company, not "less valuable." _Yes _____ No _____

- I have a reputation at work for being someone who sacrificially helps others succeed without needing any credit for it.

  _Yes _____ No _____

- My coworkers see me as a person settled, engaged, and fulfilled in my workstation. _Yes _____ No _____

- I am as energized in my work life as I am in my ministry world. _Yes _____ No _____

- I am the same person on Monday at work as I am Sunday at church. _Yes _____ No _____

- I have learned to stand firm in my convictions regardless of the setting or circumstance. _Yes _____ No _____

- My life is enough salt and light to cause my coworkers and neighbors to find Jesus. _Yes _____ No _____

- Even if I became independently wealthy, I would still keep working. _Yes _____ No _____

- I am actively helping the leadership in my church to better understand and engage the workplace. _Yes _____ No _____

If you answered yes to:

  9–10 Your Life@Work sword is a doubly sharp penetrating presence.
  6–8 Your blade is dull.
  3–5 Your blade is still broken.
  0–2 The enemy has stolen your sword.

CHAPTER I

REFORGING OUR FRAGMENTED LIFE@WORK

IT IS NOT, TRULY SPEAKING, THE LABOR THAT IS DIVIDED; BUT THE MEN: DIVIDED INTO MERE SEGMENTS OF MEN—BROKEN INTO SMALL FRAGMENTS AND CRUMBS OF LIFE.

—JOHN RUSKIN

Charles Antonio Bordini III was just being himself: high-spirited, uncomfortably transparent, and voraciously hungry to learn.

I had met Charlie for the first time the night before, at dinner. For Charlie, life is full of feeling—and moves at full throttle. He was new to Chicago and new to the life of faith. He was developing a reputation as a mover and shaker in Christian circles just as he already was in the corporate world.

If you had a large gathering of people excited about their faith—Charlie was invited. If there was a major financial deal going down—Charlie was in the middle of it. Charlie was a player. He was a player in business, and now that he was a Christian, he was becoming a player in the world of faith as well.

Seeing Charlie in action, you quickly understood why.

Hanging out with him reminds me of eating at my favorite Italian restaurant. It is loud. It is chaotic. But it is rich. The level of energy, enthusiasm, and life hanging in the air is so self-charging. As Carlos Santana said, "There is nothing more contagious on this planet than enthusiasm." Charlie is like that. He is a one-man Italian clan. In a word, he is a feast to be around. His mind is always in motion, and he wears whatever he is thinking on his sleeve.

He was now sitting across a boardroom table from me. I had just finished speaking to a large gathering of young executives over breakfast and had been asked to stick around and meet with the board of directors of the organization hosting the breakfast. They wanted me to field a few questions on the faith-and-work movement. To no one's surprise Charlie had just been added to the board.

Partway through the discussions, there was a lull. One second too long passed, and Charlie—unable to contain himself—spoke up. "I have a question," he said with confidence. "I am not sure, but I think I have a dilemma.

"A few of my employees lately have told me that there are two different Charlies that come to work. Depending upon which Charlie walks through the door, they can tell exactly what kind of day it's going to be."

With a chuckle he explained, "They told me that sometimes 'Charlie Love' shows up. Charlie Love is the Christian Charlie. He is full of patience and understanding. He cares about the bigger things in life. They like Charlie Love. When he comes to work, they know it's going to be a good day.

"But," he continued, "they also told me that there is a 'Charlie Money.' According to them, Charlie Money is all business. He walks in cracking Pharaoh's whip, driving the organization for results, pushing people, and demanding performance. He is satisfied with nothing less than excellence. Charlie Money, as you might imagine, is not so popular. When he comes through the door, everybody battens down the hatches."

Sheepishly Charlie admitted, "My folks say I am schizophrenic. To be honest, I think they're probably right, and I am not sure what to do about it."

Mike spoke up quickly in response. He was one of Charlie's Christian peers in business. "Charlie, I know *exactly* what you need to do. Charlie Love needs to drag Charlie Money down to the basement," he said emphatically, "and *kill* him!"

With obvious conviction Mike preached on: "If you can't kill him, then at least you gotta find a way to chain him down there and never let him out. That is *the* only way to survive." He even quoted a couple of Scriptures to prove his point.

People just stared at each other. The room was dead silent. You could hear the arms of the clock slowly tick off thirty seconds. Charlie sat there stunned with a puzzled look plastered on his brow. You could tell his mind was running, just trying to process what he had just been told.

Then all eyes turned to me. I, after all, had been invited to answer questions.

I hesitated, because I was not sure if they were ready to hear what I was really thinking. Finally, knowing that this was a gathering that valued truth over tact, I plunged in.

"Charlie, I could not disagree more with Mike."

Motioning toward Mike, I said, "No offense, but I simply believe our friend sitting across the table from you is dead wrong. I have another alternative for you.

"'Charlie Love' needs to meet 'Charlie Money,' and they need to get into the same skin. God wants you to learn to come to work wearing the shoes of your faith *as well as* the best business suit you have. They match. They were made to go together. You need them both on, all the time, to be all of the Charlie that God intended you to be. They need to commingle. The original blue-print of man calls for us to be capable in the world of the king-dom *and* in the world of the commercial, in beautiful and powerful concert."

Charlie Love and Charlie Money were at an impasse. Charlie Love felt called to be a person of faith, and Charlie Money felt called to make a living. Neither knew how to find the secret to being just "Charlie," a new creation made to instinctively live out God's glory and excellence in every area of life.

Does Charlie look familiar? My guess is that even though you have never met Charlie, you already know him. You have proba-bly seen Charlie in the mirror. Although Charlie Bordini is an executive, other Charlies work at all levels of the workforce.

There are Charlies in sales. Some work for supervisors, on the shop floor. Different ones work for themselves. Many work at home. Some Charlies are men, and others are women. What they all have in common is an identity crisis at work that is at epidemic levels today. We increasingly feel our work is out of sync with the rest of who we are. It is a shared predicament. At one time or another all of us feel a strain between our souls and our jobs. And harnessing those two appetites into one person is no easy task.

To be sure, we are all at diverse places on our various spiritual pilgrimages. Do you count yourself as a person of faith and a fol-lower of Christ, like Charlie? Surveys indicate that four out of ten Americans would say yes to that question. That means there are roughly over one hundred million of us out there. We all leave church on Saturday or Sunday and then on Monday hit the wall of the reality of life at work. You and I know Charlie's discomfort all too well. We go to work with it every day. For us the tightrope of being "in the world but not of it" is a daily routine.

We constantly toggle between Charlie Love and Charlie Money, never quite sure when to turn one on and the other off. Do I approach this situation as a Christian, or just as plain business? The question, what would Jesus do? is often no help, for our answer is "I wish I knew." When we try on Charlie's story, it fits.

Perhaps, however, you do not consider yourself a "Christian" per se, but in your own way you, too, value your spirituality as an important facet of your life. You also know the personal stress that comes along with this territory. You have sometimes felt that you are asked to sell your soul for your job. You want to be ethical as much as the next person; yet again and again you find yourself being confronted with potentially compromising choices. You like to think you are kind, that you care for people—you're just not sure where to draw the line in today's cut-throat business world.

You are not alone. Many feel as you do. The proliferation of books, articles, and seminars surrounding business ethics and the soft side of leadership testifies to your need. You can relate to Charlie too, and like him, you are looking for answers. Even though I work from my own Christian convictions, I think that in the pages ahead you will find much that is helpful for your own journey.

No matter what our beliefs, we are all spiritual beings. The hard, material realities of work do not exactly feed the God-side of who we are. More often than not, we perceive the demands of our employment as a stumbling block to personal balance and to the heart issues of life. We wrote this book to help Charlie Love and Charlie Money connect.

CHARLIE'S FIVE FEELINGS

Charlie lives in all of us. We are all struggling to live with the same tension as Charlie. What brings all of us "Charlies" together is that we relate to this same stressor. We are tired of straddling the fault lines transecting our lives.

This schism between Charlie Love and Charlie Money manifests itself in a number of common feelings. Which of the following do you most identify with?

"I am tired of juggling two worlds."

Neither world seems to understand or value the whole of who I am. Work says my faith is strictly personal—leave it at home! My Christian culture says that working for the world is a waste—give it up! Both are so isolated from each other. The church and the office hang out in different parts of town. They talk different languages. Yet they both demand my allegiance. I feel like a child of divorce caught in the middle of two parents. I have two different homes. Different parts of me live in each one. I want a life that is whole again. Sometimes I wish I could just get my two worlds to talk to each other!

"I need my work to have more meaning."

I want my life to count. Who doesn't? I don't want it to be a waste. Often, however, I question the value of what I do. I finish the week and, looking back, I see little that really hit me square in my strike zone and even less that will last until eternity. Sometimes it feels as if I am fighting a lost cause. In the grand scheme of things, does my job really matter? I am investing forty, sixty, sometimes even as much as eighty hours a week of my prime time and energy, but for what? For a going-away party and an all-expense-paid trip to the nursing home? If at the end of the day, that is all there is, then I will have been ripped off. That would be profoundly disappointing. That is not what I am working for. I want to work for something bigger than myself. There has to be more. Katherine Graham commented, "To love what you do and feel that it matters—how could anything be more fun?" I know one thing for sure: doing something that you feel doesn't matter definitely *isn't* fun.

> *"I need a clear picture of what being a Christian*
> *on the job looks like."*

I know that my faith should shape my work. I just don't understand what all that really looks like. We talk about a "Christian work life," but what does that really mean? Sometimes it feels and looks like an oxymoron. I know what it means to be a follower of Jesus. I also know my profession. I know who I am. I know what I have to do and what I do well. I just want to know what the two have to do with each other.

I am a practical person. I just need someone to spell it out for me. If I don't know what being a Christian looks like at work, how can I expect those around me to know what being a Christian is from my work? As the ministry sage Howard Hendricks says, "How do you convince a world that God is alive? By His aliveness in your life, by His work in producing reality in your experience." But if I do not know what God should look like in my work, how will others see Him *through* my work?

> *"I need a faith that makes a difference*
> *in my life and my job."*

I believe that following Jesus should touch every area of my life. I am committed to His being Lord of all that I am. I work in an office culture that at its worst is hostile to God, and at best, indifferent. Every day I face the daunting challenges of navigating a minefield of obstacles, any one of which could sink my career tomorrow. I cannot overcome them on my own. Frankly, my work life needs all the help it can get. If my faith can't help, then what hope do I have?

I want my life to be of one piece, but I have never seen what that looks like. That is a problem, because as the theologian Matthew Henry said, "Those who teach by their doctrine must teach by their life, or else they pull down with one hand what they build up with the other."

> *"I feel I am not receiving any help to*
> *bring my two worlds together."*

It seems as if I am all by myself in this. I wish my church would help me more, but my work life is simply off their radar screen. Too often it seems clueless about the real problems I face Monday to Friday. Every once in a while I will hear a sermon exhorting me to be more Christlike at work or encouraging me to be a more active witness, but it seldom goes deeper than that.

When I do hear about work from church, it is usually couched around working in the church. But that is *not* where I work every day. I need some help from someone who has traveled this road before me. Like Charlie, I feel as if I have dual personality disorder. How do I bridge the gulf between these two significant parts of my life?

COMMUTING BETWEEN
TWO WORLDS

Reconnecting these worlds is the heart of this book. What I told Charlie that day is one of my deepest-held convictions: people of faith must learn to be *comfortable, valuable,* and *intentional* in two worlds: the world of the kingdom and the world of the commercial, the world of faith and the world of work. That is what Life@Work is all about.

We must learn to be *comfortable* in these two worlds because we were made to live seamlessly in both. They are both our natural habitats. This world we live in was created both as a place of work and a place of worship. The naked truth is that Adam and Eve were totally at home working in God's presence.

Too often people of faith have a sense of restlessness that translates as "I just am not satisfied and comfortable with my calling and assignment connected to my work." They are always staring out the window, dreaming of the perfect job. Naturally it is at all times something different from what they currently are doing.

Kate Clinton observed that there is no contradiction between life being enjoyable and its being meaningful. She wrote, "[A] friend told me that each morning when we get up we have to decide whether we are going to save or savor the world. I don't think that is the decision. It's not an either or, save or savor. We have to do both, save and savor the world." What she said is true of work as well. To see someone relaxed in the clothing of the commercial enterprise, walking with the determined step of "I know why I am here," is so refreshing.

Today the tension between faith and work is also a tug-of-war over *value*. Commerce defines itself in terms of salary, profit, stock value, net worth, value-added, cash flow, generated income, and what I bring to the organization. Churchdom utterly rejects this economy in favor of accruing eternal significance, building a monopoly of souls, and maximizing heavenly gain.

Christ's life, however, demonstrates a contribution to both the material advancement of life on earth and the spiritual advancement of God's everlasting kingdom. He worked in the marketplace, crafting in wood and meeting human needs, *and* in the spiritual realm, providing a solution to mankind's spiritual needs on a wooden cross. As bizarre as it may be to us, God valued both of these aspects of Jesus' life equally. To live as He did, we need a convincing rationale for our value in both spheres as well.

This kind of resynthesis, however, requires *intentionality*. We must be targeted in our involvements in kingdom and commerce. Our faith is not a random commitment and neither should our work be. Intentionality of holistic living means being all of who I am and the best of who I can be at church, home, and work.

A DOUBLE-EDGED LIFE@WORK

If Charlie could have lived in J. R. R. Tolkien's imaginary age of Middle Earth, I am sure that he would have been recruited to be a member of the Fellowship of the Ring. His colorful personality was just the type that would have fit in well with Tolkien's menagerie of dwarves, elves, men, and wizards.

In *Lord of the Rings*, evil was incarnate in the Ring, a cursed gold band that Frodo works to destroy throughout the tale. The most potent symbols of hope, however, were the broken shards of a double-bladed broadsword that had once belonged to the last rightful king of Gondor. Sauron, the malicious black spirit, had killed him. He then broke that blade and terrorized Middle Earth ever since.

Nonetheless, the shattered pieces of that famous sword were rescued and preserved by the elves until the final War of the Ring. When Frodo's fellowship of merry warriors began moving against Sauron's forces, the elves reforged the fragments into a whole sword once again.

Frodo's friend-in-arms, Aragorn, was the last surviving heir of Gondor's royal line and thus the only one qualified to wield the fabled sword. Only when Aragorn accepted the reforged sword, reclaiming his true identity, was he able to marshal the forces needed to defeat Sauron. In the end the sword triumphs, the ring is destroyed, and Aragorn is restored to the throne of Gondor, reestablishing peace among men.

Each of us is the rightful heir of a stolen realm. A spiritual pretender haunts our lands, dead-set on thwarting our God-given birthright to this earth. To destroy his power we have been called to enter into a fellowship with the one true sovereign and personification of all that is good, God Himself.

God has given each of us a sword. It is a blade with two edges, representing our two destinies. One is the edge of our faith, our calling to know God intimately and then harness that belief system into the details of our lives. The other edge is that of our work. As I use my commercial muscles from a heart of faith, I incarnate God's effectual presence where I work, thus making a doubly sharp sword.

Living a life at work that cuts both ways makes you what our late friend Bob Briner called a "roaring lamb." Briner declared, "It's time for believers to confidently carry their faith with them into the marketplace so that our very culture feels the difference." It takes both Charlie Love and Charlie Money to do that. Does your work life roar?

This book is designed to help you do just that. Its goal is a double-edged life at work, a life that is razor sharp, spiritually and professionally. Abraham Lincoln once declared, "If I only had an hour to chop down a tree, I would spend the first forty-five minutes sharpening my axe." This book is to help you make every swing count.

People of faith must learn to be comfortable, valuable, and intentional in two worlds. In these two arenas rage all of the battles of the heart. Between them are caught most of the big issues of life. Charlie was right to speak up. He had his finger on a fatal fissure in life. The truths contained in the pages that follow helped Charlie reforge his work life and wield its twin-cutting blade with great finesse. These truths have the power to transform your Life@Work as well.

CHAPTER 2

WORKING IN PARADISE

THROUGH CLEVER AND CONSTANT APPLICATION OF PROPAGANDA,
PEOPLE CAN BE MADE TO SEE PARADISE AS HELL, AND ALSO THE
OTHER WAY AROUND, TO CONSIDER THE MOST WRETCHED SORT
OF LIFE AS PARADISE.

—ADOLF HITLER

When you think of the word *paradise*, what comes to mind?

Perhaps you see yourself sitting on a beach, cold drink in hand, sun on your face, breeze in your hair, a good book in your lap, and turquoise blue waters as far as the eye can see.

Maybe it would instead be lying under the stars in the Rockies, a spring-fed river running nearby, filled with tomorrow's trout, your family asleep, and a campfire popping with flames as lazy and silver orange as the full moon.

One final try: Monday morning, behind a desk with the ringing phone, a frozen computer, and an unsmiling assistant—if you are lucky enough to have one—who happens to be asking you for time off, while papers spill onto the floor and the boss wants to see the finished presentation in exactly fifty-seven minutes and thirty-three seconds.

For most Americans the ideas of work and paradise are as related as bobsledding and Jamaica. They might as well be antonyms, buzzing with the opposing energy of an oxymoron: *freezer burn, jumbo shrimp,* and *working paradise.* In fact, most of the cultural perceptions of paradise are strikingly marked by the *absence* of work: travel brochures, retirement magazines, and lottery advertisements. We are led to believe that work is at best either a chore or a way to pay the bills.

A NEW BEGINNING

As designed by God, work was not just something for men and women to *do,* like a kind of mandatory cosmic aerobics class; but amazingly, He designed it to be a deep participation in the life and work of God Himself. The purpose was to "take care" of the earth, to steward it. We are entrusted with taking care of God's resources in the same manner He would. That mandate for work did not change after the Fall. Man's continued stewardship is the lynchpin of understanding a theology of work.

That does not mean, of course, that every workday feels like "paradise." We still have to deal with the thorns that have grown up since man's fall in the garden. Even the most energized Life@Work has tough Tuesdays and frenetic Fridays. It is not the circumstances of my day, but my seizing the workday as a God appointment that stages a fresh return to paradise.

FOUR BROAD LANDSCAPES OF LIFE OR FOUR BROAD REGIONS OF PARADISE

If human society is a garden, then there are four institutions that must be nurtured for holistic health. From the earliest scenes of creation we see God designing separate structures for people to explore life. What are the Four? In addition to the worlds of *family, government,* and *church,* God has created *work* for us to discover, explore, and cultivate for His glory.

Many followers of Jesus have access to a great deal of information about three of those institutions—the church, the government, and the family. We understand that the church is nothing less than the body of Christ, directed by God to love Him, each other, and the lost.

The need for strong families has received a great deal of attention in recent years with the rise of such invaluable ministries as Focus on the Family, Promise Keepers, and FamilyLife Today. Clearly, God mandates the investment of our lives into the lives of our spouses and children.

Christians, too, have a civic responsibility. In his book *The Church of Irresistible Influence* (Grand Rapids, MI: Zondervan, 2001), Robert Lewis makes a persuasive case for Christians and their churches to reengage their communities and their cultures. Art, media, and education all need involved Christians. Unemployment, illiteracy, teen pregnancy, homelessness, health care, dissolving families—these are just some of the issues begging the church to step up its involvement, right where you and I live. For too long, evangelical Christians have been passive citizens, benefiting from society but not making a constructive contribution to it.

Politics, of course, would be the one exception. Many believers are active in government, working diligently for the passage of laws and the reliance of the protective arm of the state. There are many issues on which Christian voices need to be heard and counted. Effective democratic governance is a gift that Christian civilization has given to the world.

But what about work? What sermons have we heard lately about the inherent value and beauty of work? What books have you read lately that celebrate the "God-ness" of a good day's work for a good day's pay?

Mysteriously, a puzzling silence surrounds the God-ordained

institution of work, often leaving modern-day explorers disoriented and bewildered. "God has created me to do him some definite service," Catholic thinker John Henry Newman wrote. "He has committed some work to me which he has not committed to another." If that is true, then why does the church say so little about it?

Because this territory has been so long neglected, in many ways it is now an overgrown wilderness. The journey toward an effective, fulfilling Life@Work is not for the weak-kneed and fainthearted. As Charlie Bordini discovered, it can be unforgiving terrain. Unfortunately, the traditional sources for faith-based answers to life's dilemmas often fail to help. When mentioned at all, work generally is viewed as negative, something that keeps us from spending our time and energy on truly *important* issues—family and church.

WORK IS A MISUNDERSTOOD TERRITORY

Ferdinand Magellan lived in a time when many people still believed the earth was flat. According to this mind-set, if you sailed for too long in any one direction, you and your ship would cruise right off the edge and into the fire-filled, bottomless pit of hell. Neil Armstrong set foot on the moon in an era when many thought space exploration was a violation of God's command to "inhabit the earth." Our Life@Work is no less shackled by the chains of misconception. Consider these commonly held myths connected to work:

MYTH 1: WORK IS A FOUR-LETTER WORD

Work has a bad rap.

The conventional wisdom is that work is a necessary evil to the comforts of the American dream. It was Ronald Reagan who quipped, "It's true hard work never killed anybody, but I figure, why take the chance?" We grudgingly put in our time so that we can collect at the end of the week or month. The prize is all the rewards our consumer economy has to sell us.

This popular attitude has a spiritualized version as well. It is the assumption that work is part of the curse of the Fall. Christians think of it as a penal sentence that God delivered in anger after Adam and Eve directly disobeyed Him in the Garden of Eden. Those who embrace this myth see work as a career-long punishment that all of us—past, present, and future—must endure because Adam and Eve bought into Satan's great lie. The truth is that work was one of God's first assignments for Adam. It was part of the creation that God said is "very good."

God had already ordained work before the Fall. Genesis 2:15 reads, "The LORD God took the man and put him in the Garden of Eden to *work it and take care of it*" (emphasis added). The time frame is critical. That was chapter 2. Sin does not enter in until chapter 3. Work is not a result of sin. Work was part of God's original creation. Like the family, work is "a creation ordinance"—a potential blessing and a divine assignment.

Myth 2: Work Is Enemy Territory

According to this presupposition, work is worldly. It is part of the secular system. It is the opposite of the sacred world that we are to *really* be about. "God stuff" includes such things as prayer, Bible study, worship services, and our donations of time and money to worthy "ministries." Work is a secular and dirty pursuit.

This approach is totally counter to Scripture. This dichotomy—this split between the sacred and the secular—does not occur in God's Word. In fact, Scripture spends a good deal of ink and paper making the point that these two should be tied together—that work is part of God's everyday involvement with people.

Myth 3: Work Is Salvation

For people who buy into this myth, work becomes God. They don't go to work; they go to Work. They don't seek success; they seek Success. They don't have ambition; they have Ambition. Their entire identity becomes wrapped up in their jobs.

This is a particularly dangerous side of a "work is the family" culture, which is so much a part of the New Economy. Many organizations, religious or otherwise, sell a family-style corporate culture as a benefit. And it can be. People who take this idea to the extreme can become emotional and spiritual prisoners to their jobs. The difference between what we called workaholism in the eighties and feeling passionate about your work in the new millennium is one of motivation. Workaholism has no place in an effective Life@Work. The truth is that work is a great environment in which to discover God and glorify God, but it is *not* God.

MYTH 4: WORK IS THE LAST PRIORITY

Many followers of Christ, if asked to list their priorities, would order them this way: God, family, self, and work. Teddy Roosevelt said, "Far and away the best prize that life offers is the chance to work hard at work worth doing." By making work our last priority, we imply that it is not worth doing. No wonder so many of us feel we got stuck with a booby prize because we were not called into ministry. The fact is, an integrated, holistic view of life *includes* work. God does offer us the prize of a work that's worth doing, even if the church does not.

Consider a new set of priorities for life: God. That's it. There is no number two or number three or number four. In living out a commitment to that priority, we must make Him an integrated part of everything we do—family, self, and work. He becomes the center of the flow and the source of alignment of all the parts of our lives.

Relegating work to caboose status is as impractical as it is unbiblical. If we really put work *last*, we would not leave for work each day until we had done *everything* we should for God, family, and self. We would never earn a living! No, the truth is that work is part of a balanced approach to life and God—His Spirit, His truth, His love. When we go to work, God should not be left behind in the family Bible on the nightstand next to the comfy chair where we have our daily quiet time.

MYTH 5: WORK THAT IS ANOINTED ALWAYS SPELLS SUCCESS

There are many stories of skillful men and women who zoom up the career ladder of success. Those individuals live in the books of the Bible and on the pages of the *Wall Street Journal.* It makes sense to us when skill and success end up partnering with each other.

But then there are other accounts, stories that also appear in Scripture and in the lives of men and women we all know: people of genuine skill who do not live in the glow of a successful career. They work hard and well, and yet little career good happens. We need to make one important point as we begin our study of Life@Work: a God-filled work life does not always equate with career success. Unfortunately, many kingdom messengers offer that as the bait for folks to become more serious in pursuing a meaningful Life@Work. What Charlie is seeking is not a Christian key to unlocking worldly success, but God's key to unlocking His intended design for our work, whatever its circumstances or outcomes might be.

FOUR TOOLS FOR LIFE@WORK

I will never forget the conversation. I was sitting with a dozen businessmen around a long, wobbly table in the back room of a local eatery known for its big omelets and small prices. We gathered each week to discuss matters of life and work—and to keep the biscuit-making buddy of ours employed.

We had every stripe and age of the work landscape represented. One young fellow, early in the growth of his dental practice, threw the question on the table. "What exactly does it look like to be a Christian businessman?" Then, before anyone could even grab the question off the table, he countered with a quick follow-up to his own question. "I mean, more specifically, what does it mean for me to be a Christian dentist?" At that point the question had legs, and it was walking around the table. He did not know Charlie Love and Charlie Money from chapter 1, but he was asking the same question in a different way.

Does it mean that he should pipe in only Christian music over the airwaves floating through the office? Should his decoration be a combination of early Bible and modern Christian? Should he pay his employees more than the national average to depict a deep appreciation for their work? Or should he pay them a few bucks below the national average so they can learn to live by faith? Does he waive all receivables that are over ninety days because it is obvious those folks are having financial trouble and, as a Good Samaritan, he is here to help? Or should he hire an attorney and go after "his" money as a matter of stewardship?

That was the year when I first began to seriously look for a model from Scripture that frames the image of what it looks like for someone to be actively engaged in both the commercial and the kingdom side of life. One of the people I met in the Bible who most influenced my own Life@Work was David the shepherd-king. David's life was so significant in the history of redemption that it stretched across several books of the Old Testament and even gets mentioned a number of times in the New Testament as well.

Conventional business wisdom today says find a mentor for your work who can pull you up to where you want to go. David's life had pull. He did what we all want to do: he lived a successful life. And David's life was a success because he found and fulfilled the mission God had for him.

From a strictly human point of view, David had an impressive résumé. It was as colorful and varied as any career ladder I have ever witnessed. He overcame significant handicaps. He began as a runt in a rural family of sheepherders. In ancient societies the youngest got the least resources. They had the least privilege. They had the most work. Their education was the lowest family priority. They were given the smallest inheritance. In many ways they were on their own to make their way in the world as best they could. Family wealth and connections were spent on older siblings, not them. No one expected much out of them, except that they compliantly do the work nobody else wanted to and that they not complain about doing it. David had an uphill struggle from the beginning.

Despite the limitations of these humble origins, David's life made world history. He single-handedly killed his nation's number one, most-wanted terrorist enemy. He was hailed for the renown of his courage. He became king and united a divided kingdom.

David, however, was no one-dimensional superhero. He was human, just like you and me. He experienced life's extremes. From the picked-on baby in the family to a national hero to national laughingstock. From shepherding sheep to shepherding a nation to hiding with the sheep. From a favorite of the king to a fugitive running from the king. He was a poet who knew the joy of the Lord's anointing and the grief of a broken family. One of his sons became king and the world's wisest man. Another raped his sister. Still another tried to kill his dad.

David knew the highs of worshipping God in Jerusalem as well as the personal darkness and regret of adultery and murder. Through it all, however, David kept faithfully coming back to his God. Even though his life was littered with failures and bumps, just like all of us, Acts 13 still says that "David was a man after God's own heart and that after he accomplished all that God purposed for him, David passed on off the scene." That is a pretty good eulogy.

What could be the ingredients behind such a mission-accomplished life amid such all-too-real circumstances? In Psalm 78 we are given a telling snapshot of the work life and career of David. This passage reveals four characteristics that contributed to the success of King David's Life@Work: his calling, his service, his character, and his skill.

> [God] chose David [that is *calling*] his servant [that is *service*] and took him from the sheep pens; from tending the sheep he brought him to be the shepherd of his people Jacob, of Israel his inheritance. And David shepherded them with integrity of heart [that is *character*]; with skillful hands he led them [that is *skill*]. (Ps. 78:70–72)

Calling, service, character, and skill factors are not just unique to David but are timeless and apply to any work context. They are the essentials for every man or woman to carry into his or her work setting. Each is a crucial intersection where faith must be intentionally employed to form our work.

DAVID DELIVERED SKILL

"With skillful hands [David] led them," the psalm says (v. 72). David was skilled at what he did. He was an able leader. He was a talented soldier. And he was an accomplished musician. David was called to be king, and he delivered. He proved himself faithful shepherding sheep the same as he did shepherding a nation. David is remembered because he used his gifts for good. He built a nation. To this day, Israel is called the "house of David." David's reputation was built to a significant degree on his skill.

Faith has a corollary that we rarely associate with it. It is competency. Faith is incompatible with mediocrity. To be mediocre is to be complacent. A complacent heart is antithetical to a heart of faith. Faith gives its best, because faith is a total commitment. Faith works at delivering skill.

Skill and *faith* are two words we ordinarily would not think to put in the same sentence. Their juxtaposition raises several questions relevant to a double-edged work life. What is skill? What does the Bible have to say about it? What does God have to do with skill? Does skill really need God? What is the relationship between faith and excellence? Section one of this book explores these issues, because a successful Life@Work means you must take skill to work.

DAVID EVIDENCED CALLING

The psalmist observed that God "chose David" (78:70). David's work was directed by the evidence of God's calling. Without calling, all you have is a job. For forty-odd years you do what you can to put together the best run you can manage. You hope you can make it. You hope it matters. You hope you're headed in the right direction. It is all a crap shoot.

Working from calling, by contrast, gives you confidence in your mission. David pursued his life work out of a sense of divine commissioning. Knowing who sent you and exactly what errand you are on makes a difference. David knew what he was made for, and he knew who made him for it. He realized early on the link between battling bears and fighting giants and quickly connected the equipping by God for both.

What is calling? How do I know my calling as David did? Do I only have one calling? Does God really call people to *normal* jobs? What if I have to change careers? Is one calling better than another? How does my world change once I lock in on my calling? Section two addresses these questions, because a successful Life@Work means we must take calling to work.

DAVID MODELED SERVING

The Psalms text describes David as God's "servant" (78:70). When David went to work, he assumed a posture of service. He served his father on the family farm. He served sheep, tending and protecting them in the field. He served his people, taking on and defeating their menacing enemy. He served King Saul by ministering to him through music he played on his lyre. He served his nation, faithfully governing them as their king.

In each of these roles, however, he was most fundamentally serving his God. This was the instinct of David's work. He served. It is just what he did; but he did it for a reason. It was not random. David's identity as a servant was a function of his faith. In other words, his relationship with God defined his relationship with other people.

For David, people were not just stairs to success, meant to be treaded upon. No, people were his end users of his servant's heart. His work was not just a career advancing his own interests. On the contrary, his work was a service to others advancing their interests. David's faith meant that serving defined his work. David's Life @Work modeled serving.

What does it mean to be a servant at work? Why is serving a core issue of Life@Work? How do I grow a serving heart? What does service look like at my job? Section three deals with serving for one simple reason: a successful Life@Work means that we must take serving to work.

DAVID DISPLAYED CHARACTER

How David worked is significant. Work always has a heart, and it matters. Scripture is specific about the moral characteristics of David's track record. It says that he shepherded the nation "with integrity of heart" (Ps. 78:72). Whether we like it or not, our work is an overflow of our hearts. David's heart was fully networked with his work. He had "integrity." Integrity is the substance of good character. The character of his heart and work were good.

This was quite a contrast with David's predecessor, Saul. Saul had a divided heart. He claimed to follow God, yet he hedged his bets, allowing pagan practices as well. Saul's rule failed because it lacked internal consistency. It lacked character.

David, on the other hand, lived a transparent life. Everything was public. His work was public. His worship was public. Even when David sinned, he confessed it in public. His life was on display. His private and public lives were of one piece. He was the same with the office door closed as he was with it open. His faith brought who he was into line with what he did. The whole spectrum of David's life displayed the same character of integrity throughout.

How do we build character? What are the consequences of the character factor? Can the chasm between our public and private lives really be bridged? What does God have to offer our work on the question of character? What about my failures? Do they disqualify me from God's best? How do I go about changing my character? Section four confronts the issue of integrity, for it is imperative as people of faith who want to be successful in their Life@Work that we take character to work.

We see skill, calling, serving, and character as four universal tools that will help any and every person of faith upgrade their kingdom influence in any commercial setting. It is our firm opinion after watching the intersection of faith and work for almost thirty years that these four tools are the instruments for Charlie Love and Charlie Money to connect. In other words, we are suggesting to all people of faith: *calling*—take it to work; *serving*—take it to work; *skill*—take it to work; and *character*—take it to work.

A work life that is guided by a sense of God's calling, is known for its skill, has above-reproach character, and consistently seeks to serve others—that kind of work life is transformational. It makes waves. It will have influence. It will be noticed. It will make a difference.

WORKING ON A BREAKTHROUGH

One hundred years ago, two brothers from Dayton, Ohio, stood on the windswept dune of the North Carolina Outerbanks. Orville and Wilbur came to Kill Devil Hills to test an idea. Their wood and linen contraption sat on an iron rail, resting on a bicycle sprocket for a makeshift wheel. It was not much more than a glorified kite.

They had previously flipped a coin to see who would go first. Wilbur had won and tried first the day before. Now it was Orville's turn. Their audience was only a few curious locals who had nothing better to do, a boy and his dog, and some men from the nearby lifesaving station.

Orville climbed on and laid down at the controls. Wilbur spun the propeller. The engine caught and sputtered to life. Slowly the Wright's machine slid down the rail into the wind, gaining speed. Wilbur ran along, steadying the wing. By the time it reached the end of the rail, it was in the air. It flew. Twelve seconds, 120 feet. Man had flown. The Wright brothers had invented the airplane. It was December 17, 1903.

Darrel Collins, a ranger at the Kitty Hawk National Park, observed of their feat, "Before the Wright Brothers, no one in aviation did anything fundamentally right. Since the Wright Brothers, no one has done anything fundamentally different."[1]

What Orville and Wilbur did was master the four remaining problems of powered flight: thrust, roll, pitch, and yaw. The wing had already been innovated, thus solving the problem of lift. Men had been flying kites for ages.

A kite flying itself was another matter. That required power, a source of thrust. The Wright brothers had an advantage on the thrust issue, because they were skilled mechanics. They used their experience and resources from their bicycle business to design and build an engine that would work. Without a sufficiently light working engine, you do not have a powered flight machine, only a glider.

The three remaining problems were all about directional control. These had proved the most daunting to past attempts at flight. An airplane has to control three axes of movement at the same time. *Pitch* is the up or down movement of the nose. *Roll* is the banking of the wings up and down. *Yaw* is the horizontal control of spinning left and right.

Pitch and yaw were fairly straightforward. Just as in a ship, a rudder could be used to control left and right yaw. A flap, a rudder turned sideways, could be employed to control up and down pitch. The most difficult was roll. How do you keep the wing tips level so that the plane does not roll over?

The breakthrough came one day when Wilbur was handling a long, thin box. As he twisted it, one corner bent up at the same time the other corner bent down. Seeing its parallel sides warped with the twist gave him an idea. What if you could warp the parallel wings in the same way? Could you intentionally distort the wings to compensate and control a plane's tendency to corkscrew? Using wires, the brothers found a way to twist their wings back and forth in coordinated opposite directions, consequently solving the problem of roll.

Just as in flight, there are four crucial variables to your Life@Work: calling, skill, serving, and character. Calling is your understanding of your divine job assignment. Skill is the unique set of abilities God has given you to fulfill your calling. Serving is the fundamental posture of your work toward others. Character is what binds it all together, the vital necessity of integrity and consistency in all of who you are, in all that you do. You will never truly find your wings until you master these fundamentals. Follow them and you will learn to fly. Your work life will never be the same.

SKILL@WORK

A good friend of mine loves to watch the Saturday afternoon show *The Yankee Woodshop*. He himself is an amazing carpenter and could very well host the show. It is astonishing to me to see a pile of lumber turned into an heirloom mahogany china cabinet in just under thirty minutes on the show.

On one episode someone asked the master cabinetmaker how long it took to learn how to do that. The cabinetmaker answered, "Any ten-year-old could do it—with twenty years of experience."

The same is true for excellence in our on-the-job skills. We all would like to be the best at what we do, but few are willing to do what it takes to get there. Faith, however, calls us to the highest standard in all aspects of our lives and work. Scripture has a great deal to say about skill, but for some reason we do not hear much about it as Christians. It is funny that Jesus was a craftsman, yet skill is rarely associated with Christian faith.

Sadly, the result is that, though churchgoers have a reputation around the office as nice, honest people, they are not considered in the top of job rankings.

Yet Scripture *challenges* followers of Christ to raise the bar in their work, not lower the curve. This section will show you how to raise the bar.

SKILL

*is understanding something completely
and transforming that knowledge
into creations of wonder and excellence.*

CHAPTER 3

SKILL IS IMPORTANT TO GOD

'TIS GOD GIVES SKILL, BUT NOT WITHOUT MEN'S HAND. HE COULD NOT MAKE ANTONIO STRADIVARIUS'S VIOLINS WITHOUT ANTONIO.

—GEORGE ELIOT, AKA MARY ANN EVANS (1819–80)

Landing a Boeing 747 in Hong Kong was one of the ultimate tests of an airline pilot's skill. Surrounded on three sides by water, the old Kai Tak Airport was as close as you could get in commercial aviation to making an aircraft carrier–style landing. Only it was worse—because carriers are not surrounded by mountains. No other final approach in the world was as hairy as Kai Tak's.

As you fly in nearer, you see why. Out the window is Hong Kong's urban mass of high-rise buildings wedged on a small sliver of land between the surrounding peaks and the South China Sea. Like grass in a concrete crack, Hong Kong, with its six and a half million people, had nowhere to grow but straight up.

Dense blocks of apartment buildings stretch almost to the very edge of the airport tarmac. Boxed in by the city, Hong Kong had to reclaim land from the ocean to make the runway long enough. It extends eleven thousand feet straight out into the Hong Kong harbor. Rimming the entire scene is a range of precipitous peaks whose steep slopes surround Hong Kong like a bowl.

Landing in that bowl means that a plane has to drop from 1,800 to 675 feet in two minutes. The landing gear is down, and the flaps are extended. At first it appears that the plane is going to crash straight into a mountain. All of sudden, the pilot banks into a thirty-degree hard turn, spiraling down. It is unnerving. If you are on the right side of the airplane, you find yourself looking down directly into apartment windows.

In the final thirty seconds of flight, the pilot must level out the airplane, center it on the runway, touch down, and stop its careening 540,000 pounds before it runs off into Victoria Harbor.

Growing up in Hong Kong, I lived two miles from the end of the Kai Tak runway, directly under the flight path. Landing lights for the final approach were on the roof of the apartment building next to ours. It was against the law to fly kites, because they could get tangled in the landing gear. A friend of mine with a good arm claimed he could hit airplanes with baseballs from our roof.

It was an awesome thing to see, hear, and feel those huge jets thunder overhead, just a few hundred feet off the ground. One right after another, they came in, only minutes apart. No matter how many thousands I had already seen, I always had to watch the next one. Only the most skilled pilots are allowed to fly into Hong Kong.

THE WONDER OF SKILL IN ACTION

Skill in action is a wonderful thing to behold. Human beings are amazing. Thomas Edison said, "If we all did the things we are capable of doing, we would literally astound ourselves." Just think of all the incredible things that the human mind has thought up and that human hands have achieved: the pyramids of Giza, the Great Wall of China, the Faberge eggs of czarist Russia, the many human feats of the Olympics, landing on the moon, just to name a few. God has made us with incredible capability.

Skill, however, is not the limited domain of extraordinary genius. As Booker T. Washington observed, "Excellence is to do a common thing in an uncommon way." We know skill happening when we see it:

- a mechanic who finds and fixes a problem that no one else could locate or solve

- an entrepreneur who creates a successful business from nothing

- a professional truck driver who deftly maneuvers a fifty-five-foot eighteen-wheeler into a hard-to-get-to freight dock with only inches of leeway on either side

- a tenacious salesman who negotiates through almost insurmountable obstacles to close a tough deal

- an artist who brings living color out of a blank white canvas

- a writer who arranges words and images to make a reader's blood boil, his heart laugh, or his mind reflect

Our work is like a piece of art. There is beauty in it. Even its simple tasks are marvels. What we do is the pinnacle achievement of creation. Even our simplest tasks are unmatched in the animal world. Computers and machines struggle to do things that even a child takes for granted.

When we watch someone accomplish a task with real skill, we are simply amazed. Eugene Ionesco observed, "The end of childhood is when things cease to astonish us." There is a child in all of us that is amazed by how things work. We think, *Wow! That was really something! How did she do that?*

Astonishingly, there is little on the business bookshelf written on the topic of skill. We have not sufficiently reflected on this core aspect of our work. As we do, we begin to ask a different set of questions: What does it mean to have skill, to be exceptionally good at something? How does one become a "standout performer" in a given task? We love to see skill in action, but what is it exactly? What is skill, really?

THE SKILL OF A GOLIATH

In conventional usage, by *skill* we usually mean "expertise" or "proficiency." Christopher Zeeman defined it this way when he wrote, "Technical skill is mastery of complexity." Our skill set is our collection of competencies, what we can do. The category of skill, however, involves more than masterful execution. This bare utilitarian conception of skill is a fruit of our despiritualized view of work.

If skill is just what I can do, then what sets me apart is the degree to which I can do it better than others. As a result, skill in our culture too often ends up as a competitive weapon of destruction. It is what enables me to beat out the person at the desk next to me.

Today's corporate culture is "Exhibit A" of skill run amok. It is the dysfunctional dynamic of social Darwinism: the "survival of the fittest." I sharpen the edges of my skill to fend off the other job applicants. I brandish my prowess to establish dominance before the next promotion comes around. I humiliate the competition by closing the deal right out from under them. I thus survive to live and fight another day. Skill is the cunning that enables you to get away with as much as possible without getting caught.

This amoral outlook is fundamentally a pagan approach to skill. It is the skill mentality of Goliath, the Philistine giant who defied the army of Israel until David killed him with a slingshot and a stone. Goliath warred based on brute strength:

> Then a champion came out from the armies of the Philistines named Goliath, from Gath, whose height was six cubits and a span. He had a bronze helmet on his head, and he was clothed with scale-armor which weighed five thousand shekels of bronze. He also had bronze greaves on his legs and a bronze javelin slung between his shoulders. The shaft of his spear was like a weaver's beam, and the head of his spear weighed six hundred shekels of iron; his shield-carrier also walked before him. He stood and shouted to the ranks of Israel and said to them, "Why do you come out to draw up in battle array? Am I not the Philistine and you servants of Saul? Choose a man for yourselves and let him come down to me. If he is able to fight with me and kill me, then we will become your servants; but if I prevail against him and kill him, then you shall become our servants and serve us." (1 Sam. 17:4–9 NASB)

Goliath reveled in his dominance of the field. He audaciously challenged all comers. He relied on his physical supremacy to win. To him, might equaled right. To a Goliath, skill is a zero-sum game. It is gladiatorial. There is a winner and there is a loser. If I am successfully skilled, it means you are not. If you are successfully skilled, it means I am not. If I can beat you, then you have to serve under me. Raw, unharnessed, pagan skill has changed little since the beginning of time. What once was measured in scalps is today measured in pay stubs, client accounts, and corporate takeovers.

Have you ever seen what little boys do when they walk by a huge sandpile on a construction lot? It is instinctual. Their eyes meet. All it takes is a glance and a smile. In an instant the challenge is made and taken up without a word. The next move is a blur as both race to the top, sand flying in all directions.

They claw up the pile, trying to be the first to stand and claim the title of "King of the Hill." The winner glares down on the other still struggling to make it up. He gloats in the victory of his ascent to glory. But only for an instant, because here comes the challenger. He lunges at the king of the hill, grabbing for leg and limb. There is a struggle. The first one up loses his balance and rolls down the slope. Quickly, the challenger takes his place. A new king has been crowned.

Our work world can be like that. It is still the same old game of king of the hill. Whether one spends the week on the factory line or the front office, for many, work is a never-ending game to fight to the top of the pile. And if I only win by dethroning you, then so be it.

David Sarnoff was not far from the truth when he said, "Competition brings out the best in products and the worst in people." Those who make it to the top last only long enough to become the target of the next challenger on his or her way up. Those who live by the sword, die by the sword.

These are warriors of business survival. They do not build people. They beat people. They have to. That is how they survive. This is not what we mean by skill here. This is raw pagan savagery, only played out on a more civilized field of business.

Yes, such giants have unparalleled skill. They have mastery. They have a reputation for their exploits, but their fruit is fundamentally destructive. Sir Max Beerbohm observed that "to destroy is still the strongest instinct in our nature." When skill is the slave solely to self, the long-term result is not growth, but decay.

Skill is a sail that needs a rudder. Thomas Merton was dead-on when he said, "Unless we develop a moral, spiritual, and political wisdom that is proportionate to our technological skill, our skill may end us." This last decade of corporate America's legacy as an era of corruption only punctuates that fact.

A BIBLICAL VIEW OF SKILL

The biblical picture of skill is quite different. God created skill to be a mastery that at its heart is constructive and creative. It is the weapon not of unhealthy competition, but of commitment to the welfare of others. It was Ralph Waldo Emerson who said, "Talent for talent's sake is a bauble and a show. Talent working with joy in the cause of universal truth lifts the possessor to new power as a benefactor."

It is not competition itself that is bad, but competition without a moral compass. Competition is the foundation of both democracy and capitalism. Both use competition to maximize the common good. Lack of competition is not the answer. The former Communist world was a tragic experiment that proved that. Just as in George Orwell's novel *Animal Farm*, in Communist societies where everyone was equal, it was the party members who were "more equal" than others.[1] Egalitarianism does not end the game; it just moves it to a different arena.

The faith perspective of work does not eliminate competition. Quite the reverse, Charlie is a competitor. He plays at the top of his game. He does his best. He drives for the best price. He seeks to make his business the best it can be. He does not do so, however, as a Goliath. He does so as a David, someone who passionately pursues his calling in harmony with the goodness of God. Alexander Pope remarked that "the same ambition can destroy or save." Goliath used his brute might to decimate nations. David used his talents to build a nation.

The Old Testament word for *skill* comes directly from the Hebrew word *to know*. But the kind of knowing that it is related to does not indicate a mere superficial understanding of something. It literally means to know completely and thoroughly. It is the same Hebrew word used in the Old Testament to describe sexual intimacy between a husband and a wife: "And Adam *knew* Eve his wife; and she conceived, and bare Cain" (Gen. 4:1 KJV, italics mine). The word for *skill* describes knowing something intensely, exhaustively, and entirely.

The biblical definition of skill, however, goes beyond mere knowledge, comprehensive as it may be. In addition to knowing something completely, skill also implies the capacity to translate knowledge into something of great value. According to Scripture, a skillful person is not necessarily someone who just has a long résumé of competencies. Rather, a person of skill is an individual who has a depth of understanding linked to an ability to take that knowledge and turn it into something of significant worth. As Leo F. Buscaglia said, "Your talent is God's gift to you. What you do with it is your gift back to God."

Skill is often paired with words like *craftsmanship* and *fine workmanship*. There is no craftsmanship where there is no craft as an end product. Godly skill is always creative. It is constructive. It is a giver, not a taker. It makes a contribution beyond itself. We define it this way:

> Skill is understanding something completely and transforming that knowledge into creations of wonder and excellence.

According to Scripture, skill is *knowing*, combined with the ability to *do*. It is *deep knowledge* in sync with *fine accomplishment*. Skill is the *best theory* blended with *unsurpassed practice*. When we operate with genuine biblical skill in our jobs and careers, people are literally taken aback. Even when they are not sure how to explain what just happened, they sit up and take notice. Skill for followers of Christ is of that wondrous variety.

GOD AND SKILL

This kind of skill is important to God. Skill matters to God, because excellence is fundamental to who He is. It is at the core of His character. God is defined by His holiness. Holiness means that God is perfect in all His ways. It is His *excelling* itself that makes God unique.

In other words, His excellence is what makes God, God. Psalm 86:8 observes, "Among the gods there is none like You, O Lord; nor are there any works like Your works" (NKJV). Moses agreed, asking, "What god is there in heaven or on earth who can do anything like Your works and Your mighty deeds?" (Deut. 3:24 NKJV). He is God because there is none like Him. He is the standard. His level of skill is the benchmark.

God excels at every good thing. When David contemplated how God made him, he wrote, "I will praise You, for I am fearfully and wonderfully made; marvelous are Your works, and that my soul knows very well" (Ps. 139:14 NKJV). Since God is the connoisseur of all things good, He cannot help but delight in Himself since He is the best there is.

THE EXCELLENCY OF GOD

Appreciating the "excellency" of God is fundamental to understanding the place and value of skill in the universe that He created.

God's excellence, however, is more than just exceptional execution. It is not just perfect performance. The excellence of His skills, His capabilities, and His attributes does not consist merely in their superior quality or lack of defect. Excellence always has a moral dimension. It is consummate capability allied with moral beauty and goodness.

Every one of God's actions is a conscious consent to goodness. Psalm 145:17 explains, "The LORD is righteous in all His ways" (NKJV). Every aspect of who He is and every one of His works—all are in perfect harmony. They are perfect in their moral coordination. Everything about Him works perfectly together for the good of all. God's skill is the cosmic symphony of His love in action.

God is, therefore, the archetype of skill. His "excellency" is paradigmatic. It was fundamental to understanding all other truth. This is especially true when it comes to how we think about our work. God made creation by the pattern of His own character. He is the template by which the rest of cosmos was cut. God's excellency is woven into the fabric of the world around us. You can see it in everything. Creation is a thing of excellence, and it was made by God to be worked with excellence.

Excellence in our work matters because God made us in His image. Human beings carry the *imageo dei* in a way that the rest of creation does not. While the remainder of nature fulfills its role by created instinct, we have a capacity to voluntarily appreciate and imitate God's excellence. He gave us the ability to choose to do our best. Our work becomes worship when we willfully give out our best every day for the good of those around us through our jobs.

A salesman heads out into his territory. He has a long list of customers to call on. The first puts him off—again. The second is in a meeting, hence, unavailable. The salesman spills coffee on his tie on the way to his third stop of the day. His boss calls on the cell phone to remind him of his performance review next week. It would be easy for him to plow ahead just in a survival mode. But his favorite worship CD reminds him that God is there riding with him. He reflects on the excellence of God in the day's blue sky and white clouds. They remind him that his workday is part of a much grander work of creation. It is part of God's portrait of glory to all those he encounters. He is motivated by his God to do his best. He makes a contribution to others in all he does: his ability to listen to customers' needs, to communicate solutions, and his God-given tenacity to make sure they get delivered.

By aligning our will with the excellency of God's will, our skills become moral channels for enjoying God by imitating His excellence of character. When we apply excellency of skill to a task—whether it be a product or a service—we are taking the raw material of creation and turning it into a creation of divinely inspired beauty and awe.

JESUS AND SKILL

Our ultimate example of skill is embodied in the life that Jesus lived on this earth. We do not usually picture Jesus as a Charlie Money, someone who was a high achiever. Our mental picture of Him is usually much tamer. This is the Sunday school Jesus. He was a quiet and kind of meek guy. Pictures of Him never have Him working. He was a good carpenter, but not so good that He would make other carpenters feel bad. He never made a profit. He always gave away everything He made. He was normal: not a genius, not stupid, but average. But was He *really?*

No, Jesus was skill personified. Luke records that as Jesus grew into a man, He was known for His wisdom and abilities (Luke 2:40–51). His work gained Him favor, not just with God, but with men as well. In other words, Jesus was respected. He was known for excelling. Even at a young age He had a reputation.

Long before He began His full-time public ministry, Jesus of Nazareth was also very skilled as a carpenter. The word used to describe Jesus in Matthew 13:55 and Mark 6:3 is the Greek word *tekton*. A *tekton* was someone who understood something completely and transformed that knowledge into creations of wonder and excellence. They were able to take a rough piece of wood and put it through a process of miraculous conversion. Even before He was publicly identified as the Messiah, Jesus was known as a skilled craftsman. *Tekton* pictures someone who, with a minimum of technical equipment and a maximum of craftsmanship, could make something of beauty out of very little. No, this Jesus was no anemic wimp. The real Jesus was a master of His craft.[2]

Jesus' commitment to excellence carried into His adult ministry. He healed cases where no other physician could make disease go away. He was persuasive, dominating discussions with Pharisees and doctors of the law. He was no pushover. He was quick on His feet. He put to silence those who sought to trip Him up and get Him in trouble.

Jesus was a consummate communicator. He kept the attention of crowds of thousands. He was also a master teacher. In a little over two years, He transformed a bunch of fishermen into leaders who turned one of history's largest empires on its ear. There was virtually nothing Jesus did during the three-plus years of His full-time ministry that did not demonstrate great skill.

Why was Christ driven to excellence of skill? It was not because He was a perfectionist by personality. Neither was it because He wanted to dominate the carpentry market of Nazareth. Nor was He driven to prove that He had what it takes. Christ did His best for one reason. For Him it all had to do with His spiritual relationship with God. At the end of His life, He prayed, "I glorified You on the earth, having accomplished the work which You have given Me to do" (John 17:4 NASB). Christ excelled in His work to bring glory to the God who sent Him.

THE DIVINE BALLET OF SKILL

A number of years ago as part of some research I was doing, I arranged to observe a heart bypass operation. After I had scrubbed,

I entered the operating room, sat back, and watched a choreography of skill unfold. It was a ballet of medical dexterity, with alternating parts played in smooth coordination by the whole team: two surgeons, an anesthesiologist, a nurse anesthetist, a scrub nurse, and the operator of the heart/lung machine. All knew their craft and worked together in smooth synchronization to repair the diseased heart of the patient. Although the cardiovascular surgeon was clearly in charge, the entire group labored together as if no one was boss.

There was an economy of effort and speech that exuded quiet competence among those gathered around the patient. Conversation wandered around the normal kinds of topics one would expect from folks who knew one another well on both professional and personal fronts: how the kids were doing, where vacation would be this summer, and what the latest hospital news was. But medical data related to the patient and procedure at hand trumped all other talk, even if it interrupted a description of yesterday's saga of the flat tire on the freeway on the way home from work.

God wants to work just like that in coordination with our skill. He wants our skill to be a divinely choreographed ballet, us doing our best, following God as the lead dancer. He wants it to be a thing of beauty, not of stress. He meant for it to work for good, not just work for results. He gave us our skill to be used for His glory, not ours.

Skill matters to God. It should matter to us too. Charlie Christian cares about skill, because excellence in his skills is an extension of his spiritual relationship with his Creator. He cannot be satisfied with mediocrity and still work wholeheartedly as unto God. He cannot "just get by" and still glorify God in all he does. The excellence of God matters to Charlie. It is why he worships his Lord. Charlie, therefore, pursues excellence. For him, skill is not a business necessity but a spiritual imperative.

CHAPTER 4

GOD IS IMPORTANT TO SKILL

I DO NOTHING APART FROM MY FATHER.

—A CARPENTER FROM NAZARETH

If you had traveled to Eastern Europe back when it was under Communism, one of the bizarre cross-cultural experiences for a Westerner was going to a Soviet-style department store. The most famous of them all was just off Red Square in Moscow, the huge GUM mega department store. Its name is pronounced "goom," but somehow, to an English mind the name "gum" seemed fitting. It was a huge gray minimall taking up an entire city block just like a Sears or a J. C. Penney.

The window displays on the outside were not that different from American shops. The obligatory mannequins were standing there in their rigor mortis poses, dressed and fully accessorized just as you would expect them. The colors were a little too muted, as if faded from the sun—only that is how they were made. The style of the clothing looked somewhat dated as well, like attire that you would see in a fifteen-year-old TV rerun. You felt as though you had walked through a time warp and entered a real-life retro experience.

Inside were the typical departments: domestics, hardware, shoes, fashions, etc. Unlike in America, however, all the merchandise was behind counters. These were vigilantly manned by fireplug-shaped "babushkas," older Russian women with the physical presence of NFL defensive linemen. If you dared touch something, you set them off like a Tasmanian devil. They would run at you with arms flailing, all the while screaming incomprehensible Russian invectives at your audacity to violate their domain. You would never make that mistake twice—take it from me.

While looking for the sporting goods section, you would have seen the escalators near the back of the store. As you approached, you would notice that people were randomly going both up and down on either of the pair of escalators. That is because Soviet escalators rarely moved. They were perennially broken. You could tell by the gunk built up in all of the grooves that it was permanently frozen. Really it was more of a fancy set of metal stairs than an escalator. In a multistory shopping megaplex, it was good for one thing though: a workout.

Thankfully, an escalator will function with or without a working motor. You can always climb it by yourself if you have to. It is much more productive, however, when it is powered up and operating as its designer intended. The same is true of skill.

Everyone has God-given skill. Talents and abilities are given to believers and unbelievers alike. Furthermore, skills will function to a degree even when disconnected from their maker. That does not mean, however, that their maker is irrelevant to their use. Just as skill is important to God, God is vitally important to skill.

Skill without God will never reach its full human potential. It may very well be a resounding success in worldly terms, but its work will never have the spiritual substance that it was made for. For followers of Christ, implementing skill includes an additional dimension that is unavailable to men and women who choose to do life on their own. Besides the God-given ability born in us all, God Himself comes alongside His disciples to actively sharpen and multiply the application of their skills.

A God-centered Life@Work ought to deliver skill in a way distinct from nonbelievers. A life fully integrating its faith with its work will involve God in the use of its skills. As Scripture shows, when we bring God into our Monday-to-Friday lives, the testimony of our work will increasingly have God's fingerprints on it.

GOD-SKILL VERSUS MAN-SKILL

David's debut on the public stage was so stunning a display of skill that the young shepherd was transformed instantly into the warrior legend of a nation. The David-and-Goliath epic is a familiar story of a scornful bully, his pagan provocation to God's good name, the hand-wringing inaction of God's people, and the spontaneous initiative of an unknown "dark horse." The turning point in the drama, however, was David's skill in delivering a small stone to just the right location on Goliath's temple, with sufficient velocity to cause the man-giant to fall facedown with a thud.

You may ask, what does God have to do with it? Any farm boy worth his salt can throw a rock. Who needs God to do that? You might be right . . . if you had all day . . . and a pile of rocks . . . and the ogre would just stand there until you hit him in the right spot. On the other hand, if you have just one rock and you want to kill a murderous giant, *and* live to tell about it . . . well, in that case, you better pray.

You know the story. For days the people of Israel had cowered "dismayed and terrified" (1 Sam. 17:11). When Goliath came out each day, "they all ran from him in great fear" (v. 24). Yet the crisis was over in an instant. Goliath lost his head, David was a hero, and the Israelites defeated the Philistines.

Almost lost in the drama is a short dialogue between Goliath and David, just before the Philistine went down. Up to this point all the talk had come from Goliath in the form of a taunting monologue: "This day I defy the ranks of Israel! Give me a man and let us fight each other" (v. 10). But in a unique battlefield speech, David breaks the conspicuous silence of the Israelites with a clear manifesto:

> You come against me with sword and spear and javelin, but I come against you in the name of the LORD Almighty, the God of the armies of Israel, whom you have defied. This day the LORD will hand you over to me, and I'll strike you down and cut off your head. Today I will give the carcasses of the Philistine army to the birds of the air and the beasts of the earth, and the whole world will know that there is a God in Israel. All those gathered here will know that it is not by sword or spear that the LORD saves; for the battle is the LORD's, and he will give all of you into our hands. (1 Sam. 17:45–47)

Members of the surrounding battlefield audience no doubt had different responses to David's short address. Goliath balked when he saw that challenging him was someone of such low—er . . . make that *no* military caliber. The balance of the Philistine army was probably amused by the spectacle. David's brothers were embarrassed beyond words. Everyone else on their side likely held their breath or closed their eyes. *You don't want to see this, believe me. It will be an ugly scene.*

What Goliath viewed as a contest of skill between two soldiers, David understood as a partnership between the skilled action of an individual and God's power to make things happen. Along with his sling, David had an even more significant secret weapon: his dependence on God.

David's picture of God's role in his use of skill is clear from what he told Goliath. Goliath was on his own: "You come against me with sword and spear and javelin" (v. 45). All he had was his own physical capability and the tools of war. David had himself, his slingshot, and *his God*: "I come against you in the name of the LORD Almighty, the God of the armies of Israel." To David, God's role was crucial to the outcome of the battle. He continued, "The LORD will hand you over to me . . . and the whole world will know that there is a God in Israel." David carried a sling, but he put his trust in his God. He declared, "It is not by sword or spear that the LORD saves . . . the battle is the LORD'S, and he will give all of you into our hands."

Here in sum is David's "philosophy of skill" that Goliath, unfortunately, had very little time to ponder: "You have your stuff, and I have my stuff, but besides that, I have God, and you don't. Therefore you will die." Goliath had *skill* while David had *God-skill*, which is how we will distinguish between the kind of raw skill that is available to everyone and the kind of ability that is a fully developed partnership between an individual and God.

God-skill is founded not primarily on one's own abilities, but on the capability of one's *God*. It is a question not solely of usage, but of dependence. Both David and Goliath had innate skills. Both had access to the same type of arsenals. Both had trained in their weapon of choice and had marshaled all the physical force they could muster. The difference was that Goliath was trusting in himself, while David's primary faith was in God.

THE SKILLING OF THE HOLY SPIRIT

God's Spirit plays a special role in relation to our abilities. When we come to faith, He gives to each of us one or more special roles (1 Peter 4:10). These God-empowered abilities are commonly called *spiritual gifts*. A diverse array of gifts are mentioned in the New Testament (Rom. 12:6–8; 1 Cor. 12:8–10, 28–30; Eph. 4:11). The focus of these divinely blessed capabilities is the building up of the local church, the community of fellow believers where we live (Eph. 4:12). God describes our role in the church as being like the diverse parts of the human body (1 Cor. 12). Every part, whether it be a toe, ear, tooth, eye, or arm, has a function significant to the body's health and growth. Plugging in and using your skills and special gifts in the church is an important aspect of a mature Christian life.

We also have talents that God built into us at birth. What is it that you do best? Do you relate to people well? Are you creative? Are you good with your hands? Are you a leader? Do you excel at serving others? Too often we discount these as insignificant to our relationship to God. This is a mistaken conclusion that has tragic consequences for many Christians who disregard their investment at work because they see it as not being "spiritual." It is commonly assumed, since non-Christians have inborn talents as well as Christians, that God has no relationship to these abilities that are the core of our livelihoods. Many of us who come to Christ no longer feel that our strengths matter to God.

The Holy Spirit, however, is just as involved in creating and enabling these abilities as He is our "spiritual" giftings that we get at conversion (Ps. 104:30). In Psalm 139 David marvels how the Spirit "knit me together in my mother's womb" (v. 13). These native talents and gifts are part of the very image of God within us (Gen.1:26). How, then, could the skills we use at work ever be considered less than spiritual and less connected with the Holy Spirit? In fact, our innate skill set is no less spiritual than our spiritual gifts. Both are capabilities given by God. God wants us to bring all of who we are as a living sacrifice of worship to Him (Rom. 12:1–2).

GOD-SKILL AT WORK

The Holy Spirit is just as involved helping believers on the job as He is when they contribute at church. God is not irrelevant to our innate skills. Instead, for those in the family of faith, He now wants to come alongside us at the office and infuse our skills with His empowering presence.

God's relationship to our skills is not new. It is seen throughout the Old Testament. God's instruction to Moses regarding the construction of the tabernacle is just one example of how God can come alongside one's work skills. After He gave Moses the Ten Commandments, God kept the prophet up on Mount Sinai for some additional and rather lengthy instruction, first regarding the tabernacle furnishings: "Make the tabernacle with ten curtains of finely twisted linen and blue, purple and scarlet yarn, with cherubim worked into them by a *skilled craftsman*" (Ex. 26:1, emphasis added). A few verses later: "Make a curtain of blue, purple and scarlet yarn and finely twisted linen, with cherubim worked into it by a *skilled craftsman*" (Ex. 26:31, emphasis added). Skill was important to God. His specs for the job were specific. This was to be an ISO-certified project.

Then the focus shifts to the uniform of the priest: "Tell all the *skilled men* to whom *I have given wisdom in such matters* that they are to make garments for Aaron, for his consecration, so he may serve me as priest" (Ex. 28:3, emphasis added). "Fashion a breastpiece for making decisions—the work of a *skilled craftsman*"

(Ex. 28:15, emphasis added). The skill that God is looking for is a skill that He gave. It comes from Him. He asks that we use the gifts that He originally gave us *for Him.*

But the most fascinating reference is the one in which God specifically identifies the craftsmen He has in mind for the project:

> Then the LORD said to Moses, "See, I have chosen Bezalel son of Uri, the son of Hur, of the tribe of Judah, and I have *filled him with the Spirit of God,* with *skill, ability and knowledge in all kinds of crafts*—to make artistic designs for work in gold, silver and bronze, to cut and set stones, to work in wood, and to engage in all kinds of craftsmanship. Moreover, I have appointed Oholiab son of Ahisamach, of the tribe of Dan, to help him. Also *I have given skill to all the craftsmen* to make everything I have commanded you: the Tent of Meeting, the ark of the Testimony with the atonement cover on it, and all the other furnishings of the tent." (Ex. 31:1–7, emphasis added)

Not only was Bezalel specifically chosen by God for a task, but he was also filled with the Holy Spirit for that work assignment. According to this Scripture, Bezalel was personally appointed by God. Then he was filled with the Holy Spirit specifically as a supplement to his skill as a craftsman, for the purpose of his work. Not only does God order the best skill, not only was He the one who it came from, but His Spirit continues to supernaturally enable it.

Moses then confirmed that combination of skill and God's Spirit when announcing Bezalel's appointment to the nation of Israel in Exodus 35.

> Then Moses said to the Israelites, "See, the LORD has chosen Bezalel son of Uri, the son of Hur, of the tribe of Judah, and he *has filled him with the Spirit of God,* with skill, ability and knowledge in all kinds of crafts—to make artistic designs

for work in gold, silver and bronze, to cut and set stones, *to work* in wood and to engage in all kinds of artistic craftsmanship." (vv. 30–33, emphasis added)

But Bezalel was far from unique. At a later point, Moses was struggling to accomplish all his duties as leader of God's people. He did not have time to arbitrate between all the disputes of the Israelite nation. So God had Moses appoint seventy elders to help him carry the load. God then gave His Holy Spirit to each of them to help them carry out their responsibilities.

> The LORD said to Moses: "Bring me seventy of Israel's elders who are known to you as leaders and officials among the people. Have them come to the Tent of Meeting, that they may stand there with you. I will come down and speak with you there, and I will take of the Spirit that is on you and *put the Spirit on them.* They will help you carry the burden of the people so that you will not have to carry it alone." (Num. 11:16–17, emphasis added)

In the book of Judges, there is a whole string of leaders for whom the Holy Spirit came alongside their callings to a specific work task:

- Othniel: "The Spirit of the LORD came upon him, so that he became Israel's judge and went to war. The LORD gave Cushan-Rishathaim king of Aram into the hands of Othniel, who overpowered him" (3:10).
- Gideon: "Then the Spirit of the LORD came upon Gideon, and he blew a trumpet, summoning the Abiezrites to follow him" (6:34).
- Jephthah: "Then the Spirit of the LORD came upon Jephthah . . . he advanced against the Ammonites" (11:29).

And in the book of 1 Samuel:

- David: "So Samuel took the horn of oil and anointed him in the presence of his brothers, and from that day on the Spirit of the LORD came upon David in power" (16:13).

In the New Testament, the disciples were given the task of carrying the gospel all over the world. That great commission was specifically linked with the coming of the Holy Spirit to help them fulfill that task: "But you will receive power when the Holy Spirit comes on you; and you will be my witnesses in Jerusalem, and in all Judea and Samaria, and to the ends of the earth" (Acts 1:8).

We cannot have God-skill without the Holy Spirit's help. The Holy Spirit plays an indispensable role in lifting our level of skill to accomplish the task that He has called us to. Regular skill and God-skill are not the same thing.

THE AWE OF GOD-SKILL IN ACTION

Scripture is full of the stories of men and women who display God-skill in their routine work. Sometimes it is manifested in quiet ways and subtle shades. At other times their God-skill is flamboyantly dramatic, evoking an immediate and visceral reaction from those looking on.

JOSEPH

Besides being a slave, Joseph was a resident alien in Egypt, with a rap sheet. Even as a prisoner, however, his God-skill stood out. He correctly predicted the fates of two fellow inmates. Later, the one who remained alive told Pharaoh that Joseph was able to interpret dreams.

Pharaoh had called all his magicians and wise men together to determine the meanings of two disturbing nightmares. None of them could explain the dream, so in some desperation, Joseph was hauled out of the dungeon; given a shower, a shave, and a change of clothes; and brought before the greatest ruler of the world.

From the beginning Joseph was clear to Pharaoh that he could help find the dreams' interpretations, but not in his own power. He humbly explained, "I cannot do it . . . but God will give Pharaoh the answer he desires" (Gen. 41:16). Joseph not only gave a complete accounting for everything Pharaoh had seen in his vision, but he also made extensive recommendations for a solution. He then stood quietly, and everyone waited apprehensively for the great ruler's response. It could not have been more decisive:

> The plan seemed good to Pharaoh and to all his officials. So Pharaoh asked them, "Can we find anyone like this man, one in whom is the spirit of God?" Then Pharaoh said to Joseph, "Since God has made all this known to you, there is no one so discerning and wise as you. You shall be in charge of my palace, and all my people are to submit to your orders. Only with respect to the throne will I be greater than you."
>
> So Pharaoh said to Joseph, "I hereby put you in charge of the whole land of Egypt." Then Pharaoh took his signet ring from his finger and put it on Joseph's finger. He dressed him in robes of fine linen and put a gold chain around his neck. He had him ride in a chariot as his second-in-command, and men shouted before him, "Make way!" Thus he put him in charge of the whole land of Egypt. (Gen. 41:37–43)

Joseph's God-skill was wise, accurate, and sensible. By yielding himself to God's enabling, Joseph's work life transformed Egypt and helped save his own people from starvation.

SAMSON

God chooses to use imperfect people. That is the glory of His grace. That is your and my only hope. Samson was one such flawed individual. Unfortunately for him, his flaws were public and, in the end, fatal. They did not, however, stop God from using him mightily.

God had selected Samson as one of the judges in Israel during the time between the death of Joshua and the appointment of the first king, Saul. The Holy Spirit empowered Samson, giving him unusual physical might. Scripture says that as Samson grew up, "the LORD blessed him, and the Spirit of the LORD began to stir him" (Judg. 13:24–25). God had chosen for Samson's strength to be symbolized by the length of his hair, a fact known only to Samson and his parents. His legendary locks were cut just once in his lifetime: when Samson revealed the secret of his strength to a prostitute named Delilah. She proved to be his downfall. Delilah shared this intelligence with Samson's Philistine enemies. One night they came while he was sleeping and cut his hair. When he awoke, he was powerless. They captured him, blinded his eyes, and threw him in jail.

While in captivity, Samson's hair again grew. Apparently the Philistines had short memories and forgot about the secret of Samson's strength.

One day, a large celebration was being held at the Temple of Dagon. The building was packed with all the rulers of the Philistine assembly as well as three thousand spectators on the roof. As part of the festivities, the blind Samson was brought out to entertain the crowd as a mockery. Feeling his way, Samson asked to be placed where he could lean against the huge pillars of the temple. As he braced himself between the mammoth columns, he prayed: "O Sovereign LORD, remember me. O God, please strengthen me just once more, and let me with one blow get revenge on the Philistines for my two eyes" (Judg. 16:28). To the delight—and then the horror—of those who watched, Samson pushed the pillars apart. Everyone was killed instantly, and Scripture records this epitaph: "Thus he killed many more when he died than while he lived"

(v. 30). By himself Samson was impotent, but when he relied on God, his God-skill was spectacular.

SOLOMON

Solomon had big shoes to fill as the son and successor of King David. David had a knack for governing well. He had succeeded in uniting disparate parts of the Israelite people into one kingdom. David had set the bar of kingship high. How does one follow up a legacy like that?

Solomon understood the importance of a king to the welfare of a nation, so early on he specifically asked God for "a discerning heart to govern [God's] people and to distinguish between right and wrong" (1 Kings 3:9). Facing a daunting challenge, he asked God for help. That request was not made in public; it was in the dark of night, a private interaction between a new king and his God. God answered his prayer.

Almost immediately Solomon was presented with a showcase opportunity to demonstrate what God had promised him. Two prostitutes came to him, both claiming to be the mother of a newborn child. Each had recently given birth, but one of the infants had died. Now both contended that the live boy was theirs.

The women pleaded their cases, and Solomon had a conundrum. Each of the parties was equally passionate and adamant that the child belonged to her. So Solomon asked for a sword. His solution, he told them, was to cut the boy in two and give each woman a half. The birth mother of the child could not bear the thought of her baby dying. She begged the king to simply give the child to the other woman. Solomon had slyly discerned the real motives of each and promptly gave the child to his real mother.

The reactions as King Solomon premiered on the wisdom stage? "When all Israel heard the verdict the king had given, they held the king in *awe*, because they saw that he had wisdom from

God to administer justice" (1 Kings 3:28, emphasis added). Solomon's God-skill was awesome.

JESUS

The God-man evidenced God-skill wherever He went. One day the spiritual authorities, trying to trap Him, came and asked if they ought to pay taxes to Caesar. He responded:

> "Show me a denarius. Whose portrait and inscription are on it?"
>
> "Caesar's," they replied.
>
> He said to them, "Then give to Caesar what is Caesar's, and to God what is God's." They were unable to trap him in what he had said there in public. And *astonished* by his answer, they became silent. (Luke 20:24–26, emphasis added)

Jesus' God-skill was astonishing.

Skill is wonderful to behold, all by itself. God-skill, though, is even more resplendent. At different times and in various situations, it is wise, accurate, spectacular, awesome, effective, fearful, incredible, and astounding.

GOD-SKILL IN PRACTICE

As followers of Christ, we have available to us all the power and wisdom of God Himself. God has given us His Holy Spirit to live and work in and through us. He wants to take our level of skill to heights otherwise impossible to reach. We must trust Him. It is up to us to ask for His help. Don't climb the escalator on your own power. Call on its Maker. Use it as He intended.

It is your choice to yield your skills to Him or to continue to work on your own. Your skill is important to God. And, just as important, God is important to your skill. The next time you—like David—face a giant at work, try praying something like this:

> Lord, I need You. I believe that You are here right now in battle, right beside me. Please help me overcome this. Thank You that I do not have to face this alone with my limited resources. Guide me as I seek to use my skills to the best of my ability in this situation. You are my God, and I trust in You. I yield to Your agenda. I release my control of this situation to You. I cannot do this in my own power. I need You to bless and enable my efforts. Thank You for the help of Your Holy Spirit and for hearing my prayer. Amen.

CHAPTER 5

DISCOVERING YOUR GREATNESS

WHAT I DO IS ME. FOR THIS I CAME.
—GERALD STANLEY HOPKINS

Andrew Clemens was not your probable candidate for the greatness hall of fame. He was born in America in 1857 to a destitute German family. His parents had fled from poverty in their motherland only to find that hardship continued to stalk them as refugees here. In that era, an immigrant's life was the bottom of the barrel. Immigrants had to take what work they could get just to feed their children.

Andrew's father eventually got lucky, however. He finally found his opportunity by opening a wagon shop in McGregor, Iowa, a town on the Mississippi River where settlers embarked heading west. Boatloads of pioneers came up the Mississippi to McGregor, where they got off and bought the supplies they needed to continue their trek.

Building wagons to meet that demand gave the Clemens family

the toehold they needed in the New World. Perhaps now their children could grow up and make good. Maybe they could get an education and have a life their parents never did. At least, that was the dream they were working for.

For little Andrew Clemens, however, that hope was dashed when at age five he was struck with "brain fever"—what we now know as encephalitis. Encephalitis is extremely dangerous even today in the era of modern medicine, even more so back then. Andrew almost died, but at long last he pulled through. Tragically, the fever left him deaf in both ears. Eventually his speech atrophied, and he became mute as well.

If immigrants had it hard on the eighteenth-century American frontier, those with physical disabilities had it even harder. Deaf-mute children had little future. If they were lucky, perhaps they could eke out a meager living by begging or—at best—doing manual labor. Needless to say, Andrew was not in the running to one day be a famous Iowan.

Andrew grew up playing on the bluffs of Old Man River. One day he found an exposed cliff with beautiful colored layers of sandstone. He put some of the sand in his pocket and took it home. Later he began playing with the sand, putting it in bottles and using the colors to make designs. People liked his colorful, sand-filled bottles, and soon he was getting orders for so many that it became a full-time job. The more bottles he did, the better he became. Eventually he began creating exquisitely detailed pictures: elaborate landscapes, ships and trains, even portraits. Clemens became famous for his work. He received orders from England and the Continent. People came all the way from Europe just to watch him work.

Clemens had single-handedly invented a new art form: sand art. He used no paint, no brush, and no glue—only a few crude wooden instruments and naturally colored grains of sand. The

Victorian bottles he used had domed tops and open bottoms, which meant he created his masterpieces not only in reverse, to be seen from the outside of the glass, but upside down, starting with the top layer. The weight of the packed sand was all that held the image in place.

To see one of the few surviving Andrew Clemens sand bottles is to behold a true marvel. Each looks just like a miniature painting. They are exquisitely detailed. Their colors are true to life, with depth and light created by subtle shading.

In the end, Andrew Clemens's story is not really about his limitations as a poor immigrant's son or the tragic lot of someone both deaf and mute, but it is the lesson of discovered and developed genius. Clemens worked with what God had given him: nimble hands, a creative mind, discarded bottles, and common sand from a nearby riverbank. These were his simple ingredients for making something of magnificence.

If you go to the Iowa Historical Museum and see their collection of Andrew Clemens's art, you will never doubt that he was a man who discovered his greatness. The fact that there was much that Andrew Clemens could *not* do did not matter, because he found the one thing he did better than anyone else. Here was a man who did what he was created to do. Ralph Waldo Emerson said, "Each man has his own vocation; his talent is his call. There is one direction in which all space is open to him." Clemens found the one door that had his name on it, and by going through it he discovered a whole new world of possibility.

How do you do that? How do you figure out what God made you for? How can you find and develop your unique God-given gifts amid life's hard realities and despite your personal limitations? You will never experience the Life@Work that God intended you for until you answer the question, what is my created greatness?

LIMITED EDITION

Like Andrew Clemens, you were made for greatness. When God made you, He had something in mind that He designed you to do. He built it into you. David was pondering how God made him when he wrote, "I am fearfully and wonderfully made" (Ps. 139:14). How were you "wonderfully made"? What incredible design did God weave into your inward parts? Just as Andrew Clemens carefully placed grains of sand to create a picture, God meticulously placed inside you each piece of His design for your greatness.

At creation God breathes something special into each of us. He makes us to reflect a little of the wonder of who He is. We are not gods, but according to the first chapter of Genesis we were made in the image of God:

> Then God said, "Let Us make man in Our image, according to Our likeness; and let them rule over the fish of the sea and over the birds of the sky and over the cattle and over all the earth, and over every creeping thing that creeps on the earth." God created man in His own image, in the image of God He created him; male and female He created them. (Gen. 1:26–27 NASB)

That is what makes each of us unique. We are mirrors—albeit cracked mirrors—of the image of God. This is what makes me a person and not an animal. The image of God is at least partly seen in our God-given capacity for our work on earth. David was saying that we all carry the fingerprints of God. This is what makes me special.

It is said that "you are totally unique, just like everyone else." That uniqueness varies in each of us. Just like our fingerprints, no two of us are made to work the same way. We each have a different set of custom-built wiring. This includes our personalities, our skill sets, and our motivated abilities. Some call this our "shape." It is the profile of who we are—our blueprints. You are innately programmed to do your best working with a particular style. To find your created greatness, follow your wiring.

THE LESSON OF DAVID'S GREATNESS

David was designed to be a giant-killer. God made him to take on huge challenges that no one else wanted to do. When it came time to fight Goliath, conventional wisdom told him that a giant-killer looks like a strong, well-armed soldier. He wears big armor. He has a heavy helmet. He carries a massive shield and a huge, heavy sword. This was the expectation that Saul placed on David:

> Saul said [to David], "Go. And GOD help you!" Then Saul outfitted David as a soldier in armor. He put his bronze helmet on his head and belted his sword over the armor. David tried to walk but he could hardly budge.
>
> David told Saul, "I can't even move with all this stuff on me. I'm not used to this." And he took it all off. (1 Sam. 17:37–39, THE MESSAGE)

David had to cast aside the expectations of what others thought he should be and give himself the freedom to be who God made him to be. David knew what he was designed to do. He knew what he was good at and what he was not. He was not great at carrying heavy armor. He was too small. On the other hand, he knew that he was skillful with a rock and sling. David knew he could never do what God wanted him to do wearing someone else's armor. That was not him. You cannot freely rotate your arm in a suit of iron. It was only as he gave himself the freedom to be what God had made him that he found his greatness.

You cannot wear the armor of another, either. You must find what fits you. There comes a point in each of our lives when we must brush aside the expectations of others, the pressure of parents, peers, and society, in order to find who we were truly made to be. If we don't, they will crush us.

Jenny's mom was a well-known neurosurgeon. The plan was for Jenny to go to med school and to one day take over her mom's practice. It was an unspoken agreement. Jenny liked the thought of her mom's approval, and her mom liked the pride that comes from a daughter following in her footsteps. Jenny worked hard in high school and got good grades, then succeeded in getting into the right university, her mom's alma mater. Her mom was so pleased.

Jenny's premed track was grueling. Her biochemistry major was one of the toughest, but Jenny put in the long hours required to excel. She had little time for anything outside of her studies. She knew what it would take to get into med school. Jenny struggled for motivation to press on sometimes, but she knew she was on track, so she just kept pushing.

Then came the MCAT tests. For a year Jenny took prep courses and crammed for the tests, on top of her regular honors class load. She was relieved when her scores were good. But, she still had to get into the best med school for her and her mom's dream to come true. Over summers she had done all the right internships. Her mom had helped her get the right references from her connections. It all paid off when the acceptance envelope came.

She thought she had made it. She was finally studying to be a neurosurgeon, just like Mom. Then, near the end of her first year of med school, it hit her. It was a wall: exhaustion, depression, anxiety. She had nothing left to go on. She broke down. She had to take a leave of absence. She was crushed. She would never be a neurosurgeon. That was not the tragedy, though. The real tragedy was that she had spent years wearing someone else's armor. This unnatural load broke her. She had not found what she was made for, because she never gave herself permission to ask the question.

David knew that someone else's armor would not fit him. He also knew his God-given greatness. He knew his sweet spot. God has intrinsically deposited His creation fingerprints into the soul, the inner being of all of us. But how do we find out what that is? How do we discover where our greatness lies? The answer lies in reverse engineering.

REVERSE ENGINEERING

What is reverse engineering, you ask? It is when you start with a final product and deduce backward, figuring out its original design.

One of the greatest triumphs of reverse engineering occurred during World War II. According to tradition, the decisive event that led to the victory in Europe was the successful D-day invasion. D-day would never have succeeded, however, had it not been for an earlier and less-known victory: Operation Enigma.

The battle of the Atlantic was a German U-boat effort to sink English and American ships carrying supplies for this vital reconquest of Europe. Early in the war, German subs slaughtered Allied shipping by intercepting enemy vessel coordinates transmitted over encoded radio orders. If the Allies could not get their forces and supplies across the Atlantic, they would never retake the Continent.

Enigma was the allied effort that broke the code of German encryption machines, a battle fought secretly on an English estate called Bletchley Park. Inside its ivy-covered rock walls, cryptographers worked to decode German radio intercepts. Their real break came when they received various parts and manuals for German code machines that had been retrieved from seized German ships.

Their challenge was to reverse engineer the coding process,

using the parts in their possession, to reconstruct the original radio messages. Working backward, the Allies broke the design of the German code machine, allowing them to read German radio traffic. From the intercepts the Allies were able to plot the patrol positions of German subs. With this information, the convoys of supply ships from America that were critical to the Allied war effort were able to elude the Germans. This victory in the battle of the Atlantic made possible by Enigma decoding was crucial to the success of the later D-day invasion.

We face a similar reverse-engineering challenge. God does not deliver us into this world with a label on our foreheads that reads, "Artist" or "Salesperson" or "Teacher." Part of the grand adventure of life is that God leaves it up to us to discover for ourselves what we are best at. Like Operation Enigma, discovering what you were made for requires analyzing the parts of the machine.

While there are many aspects to who we are as individuals, I want to discuss two factors especially significant to discovering our "Sweet Spot." Our point of greatness is usually found at the intersections of what we are good at and what we like to do. Greatness requires both desire and knack. Aspiration without ability will get you nowhere. On the other hand, talent without motivation will never excel either. Greatness is an amalgam of both.

GIFTING

The obvious place to start is with what you are good at. What do you do well? Discovering what you are good at takes some thought. What you are looking for is not one answer, like "I am good at sales." Rather, you are looking for all the things that *make* you good at sales: communication, networking, relating to people, etc. These are all clues. They paint a picture. That picture is not a specific job, but a composite portrait of a skill set.

Code breakers work by laying out the message to be deciphered in front of them and looking for patterns. Similarly, we need to lay out the major episodes of our work life and look for recognizable commonalities. Stop reading for a moment and take out the best tools for discovering your greatness: a pen and a piece of paper.

Down the page, list every job or task role that you have ever had. Read back over the list and think through each position. What did you learn about yourself from each one? What were you really good at in each job? Write these observations about your strengths in a second column beside each job. Finally, ask yourself what were you required to do that you were bad at? Write any weaknesses that these episodes revealed in a third column. Now write a paragraph summarizing your list:

"I like working at . . ."

"I am good at . . ."

"I know that I am not good at . . ."

As you fill in the blanks from your experience, a general picture will emerge. Your history will demonstrate a pattern. That pattern is your skill set. It is the unique package of assets that God has given you.

A creeping mind-set has been laying hold of life and work the last few years. It is that any of us can be great in anything, and the way to do that is to simply assign energy toward growing every weakness into a strength. The problem is, that just never works. Actually, the better thing to do is to find our strengths and optimize them in every venue of our life. This romance with being the super, omnicompetent person has left the majority of workers in today's marketplace feeling that their strengths are not attached to their daily life and work.

A recent Gallop study revealed that "only 20% of employees working in large organizations feel their strengths are in play every day. Most bizarre of all, the longer an employee stays with an organization and the higher he climbs the traditional ladder, the less likely he is to strongly agree that he is playing to his strengths."[1]

PASSION

Being good at something is not enough to propel you to greatness. It requires an accompanying passion as well. Bob Biehl says that when you get down to it, people do what they *want* to do. It takes "want-to." What do you want to do? Biehl is right: if you are doing what you want to do, you will arrive early and stay late. On the other hand, if your job is something that you do not want to do, you will show up late and leave early. You cannot overlook your gut desires. They are part of your God-given wiring just as much as your talents and abilities.

Doug was a people whirlwind. He didn't have to learn how to be drawn to people. He was unconsciously competent in this area. If anything, he had to learn how to govern that social desire toward balance. Doug was energized by people. He had found what he had a passion for.

Go back to your job history. As you read line by line the experiences of your work life, are there any that you hated? If so, put a line through those. You do not want to go through that again, do you? Bad work experiences are not wastes because they offer the opportunity to learn a valuable lesson. They helped you discover what you *don't* want to do. As Henry Ford said, "Failure is the opportunity to begin again, more intelligently." When you are finally saying good riddance to a job, stop long enough to identify what it is about that position that you did not like. What do you never want to do again? What can you only tolerate in small doses?

What should you avoid at all costs? The answers to these questions provide beneficial information. It is unwise to put yourself in a job where you are structured to fall short. Now you can add another summary sentence to your paragraph:

"I know I need to avoid jobs that involve . . ."

Knowing what to avoid is priceless discernment. It will save you from turning down many dead-end streets in life. Knowing what to say no to is as critical as knowing what to say yes to.

Study your past one last time. This go-round, look for the jobs that you loved. Circle them. Now ask yourself what it was about those that you liked. What challenged you? What made your heart beat? What did you get excited about? Pull these insights into another sentence for your summary paragraph:

"I am drawn toward jobs that involve . . ."

What you have created on paper is a mosaic of what you are good at and what you like to do. These are your motivated abilities. Maximizing your motivated abilities is the key to discovering your greatness. John Ruskin said it best: "When love and skill work together, expect a masterpiece."

JACK-OF-ALL-TRADES, OR MASTER OF NONE?

There are two basic mistakes that people make in relation to greatness. One is to believe that you are great at everything. If you think that you are great at everything, you are wrong. I am sure you have met the type. They have to do everything. They cannot delegate, because they think they can do it all better than anyone they know. On a team, they will take your role right out of your hands. Or at least they will tell you how *they* think it ought to be done. They do it all to prove something. For them, anything less than flawless execution on all fronts means failure, and they cannot face that. They really believe they are great at everything. If that's you . . . news flash! You're not. But that's OK; you do not have to be. God never meant us to be omnicompetent. That's His job.

The problem with trying to be a "jack-of-all-trades" is that you spread yourself too thin. As Malcolm Bane observed, "If you wait until you can do everything for everybody, instead of something for somebody, you'll end up not doing anything for anybody." You burn yourself out doing things you were never built to handle.

Have you ever made a pizza crust? You can only spread the dough so far until it develops holes. If you are trying to do everything, you'll develop holes too. They will either be holes in your job performance or holes in *you*. Your well-being cannot help but suffer when you try to do what you were not made for. You will probably be too busy to notice the holes, but I guarantee you that your coworkers and family know where they are. Just ask them. They are the ones having to come behind you and patch things up.

Only God is omnicompetent. If God made us great at everything, we would have no need for each other. Knowing what you are not good at is just as crucial as knowing your strengths. Failures can provide real dividends if we will learn their lessons well.

You are great at *some*thing. Finding it will be a process of elimination. Realistically, you need to pare down the list. You will never be great until you narrow your target. Even those people among us who are generalists are not equally great at all tasks or initiatives.

Others have a different problem. They do not believe they are great at anything. They are masters of none. This is the lie that I am nothing special. I do not have greatness. I am just average. This "all-C" grade mentality shows a lack of self-understanding.

God has given each of us a work that He specifically intended for us to do. "Every calling," Oliver Wendell Holmes said, "is great when greatly pursued." We all carry a unique facet of God's image within us. It is the fingerprint of our Maker on us. There is no such thing as a stock human being. Each of us is custom-made to God's specifications. Satan's lie is that each of us is a nobody. He wants to keep us from identifying our greatness.

Warren Buffet, the legendary billionaire investor, was addressing a room of college students. Predictably, they wanted to know the key to his success. "If there is a difference between you and me," he said, "it may simply be that I get up every day and have a chance to do what I love to do, every day. If you want to learn anything from me, this is the best advice I can give you."[2]

PROPER ALIGNMENT

It is not enough, however, just to know your motivated abilities. Greatness is only manifest when you find a job that best fits your shape. Just as every person has a definable set of motivated abilities, every job had a set of required abilities. Every position has a set of skills that are critical to its execution. It does not matter if you are the CEO of Wal-Mart, a cashier in the drive-through at Taco Bell, or the babysitter for the five-year-old next door. Every job has critical skill requirements.

Discovering your greatness comes from maximizing the alignment between your shape and your job. When my skill set matches the critical skills of my job, I am in my work-world rhythm. To the degree that job requirements fall outside my core motivated abilities, I will experience depletion as I exert the extra effort necessary to work outside what I like to do. Burnout is the unintended consequence of someone's having a lot of jobs to do that he has no wiring for.

If you are not good with numbers and you suddenly have to take on major financial accounting responsibilities, your job satisfaction will go down. If you are not good at selling but your job requires it, eventually you will find yourself emotionally depleted by working out of your weakness.

On the other hand, if there is a lot of who you are that is not tapped by your job, you will end up bored. People who are bored at work typically seek an outlet for their passion through their avocations. When you see someone who spends just as much time with Little League as he does at work, chances are he is compensating for a bad job fit. It is sad that, as Henry Louis Mencken commented, "the average man gets his living by such depressing devices that boredom becomes a sort of natural state to him." Clubs, community boards, and churches are full of volunteers who are seeking an outlet because of a bad fit at work.

Maximum job fit comes from discovering your greatness and working out of it. That is what David did:

> David took his shepherd's staff, selected five smooth stones from the brook, and put them in the pocket of his shepherd's pack, and with his sling in his hand approached Goliath . . . [Then] David reached into his pocket for a stone, slung it, and hit the Philistine hard in the forehead, embedding the stone deeply. The Philistine crashed, facedown in the dirt. (1 Sam.17: 40, 49, THE MESSAGE)

When David was slinging stones toward Goliath's forehead, he was working out of his greatness *and* the greatness of his God. David's smooth execution in his sweet spot did not come overnight. It was the product of all of his life experiences that had prepared him. David was tested and primed as a shepherd boy. In the fields, working with sheep, he learned about himself, what he was good at, what he was not good at, what he liked, and what he did not like. Furthermore, he practiced and honed his skills. David was able to kill Goliath because he had already passed the two tests of killing a bear and a lion.

Peter Drucker was dead-on when he said that you ought to build your life on your islands of strength. To do that you have to know what you are great at. John Gardner explained that "mastery is not something that strikes in an instant, like a thunderbolt, but a gathering power that moves steadily through time, like weather." The key to not drowning in the ocean of possibilities is mapping the limits of the shoreline of your capabilities.

HITTING THE RIGHT TARGET

Pelicans are not the most beautiful birds you will ever see. Their small heads are out of proportion with their long beaks and flabby gullets. They do not have particularly colorful feathers. They have squatty short legs and big webbed feet. They waddle. They look lazy. You usually see them just sitting on top of a piling.

One thing a pelican knows how to do, though, is catch fish. That is what pelicans are great at. They know their target, and they know how to hit it.

Taking to the air, a pelican steadily pumps its long wings, gaining altitude. Like a Sikorsky helicopter, the air compression can be heard with each stroke as he slowly comes closer: *wump . . . Wump . . . WUMP . . . WUMP!* Finding the wind, he begins to glide, wings now rigidly taunt as he effortlessly rides its current up and up. Then suddenly, seeing potential food, he banks hard right and down—pivoting almost on the tip of one wing.

Wings fold back as the huge bird fearlessly dive-bombs toward the water. Now in gravity free-fall, its heavy body accelerates like a missile guided by its keen eyes, dead-on its prey. Down, down,

down . . . *splash!* At the last instant before impact, it opens its gaping beak and scoops up its next meal. Before the water even settles, the pelican is back up, bobbing there, gulping down its lunch as if nothing had happened.

An incident this summer in Arizona, however, proved what pelicans are not good at. They were not made for drilling holes in asphalt. It seems that over thirty of the endangered birds were hurt or killed when they unfortunately attempted to dive into shimmering roadways. Food was scarce on the West Coast, and pelicans began flying east, looking for something to eat. Reaching Arizona, they mistook the hot roads as glistening water, with tragic results. Pelicans were never made for dive-bombing highways.

Like those pelicans, too many of us are disoriented in our careers. We find ourselves sprawled out on a highway, wondering what hit us. Yes, Christians should deliver excellence of skill. That much we agree on. But, like the pelicans, you cannot do that if you are working totally out of your element. Finding the right fit starts with assessment. It means discovering your greatness. But you cannot forget alignment. You have to find the best place to deliver what you have to offer. What were you just *made* to do?

CALLING@WORK

PEOPLE OF FAITH OUGHT TO EXPERIENCE CALLING IN THEIR WORK.

Calling, in its fullness, is an idea too good to be true, unless and until Jesus is involved in the conversation. When He calls, He does so with great precision. Not only does He know what needs to be accomplished and how that task fits within eternal boundaries. He also knows the one He is calling, because He made that person specifically to do what he or she is being called to do. Like a giant job-match service in the sky, Jesus pairs His children up with His kingdom tasks.

Jesus will not ask us to do something for which we are not equipped. Why would He create us improperly to accomplish a mission for which we are unsuited and unprepared? Jesus does ask us sometimes to do tasks that are not much fun. Daniel was supremely prepared to be the top administrator to multiple kings. They were cruel pagans, and he was a prisoner in a foreign land. All things considered, he probably would have preferred to trade some position for some freedom.

Calling need not be a lifetime mystery. God intended from the beginning to unfold His plans and desires for each us with specificity. If there is anything that ought to sound good in today's world, it is this: work can have eternal purpose, and our lives can have fullness of meaning through the work we do.

CALLING

*is God's personal invitation
for me to work on His agenda,
using the talents I have been given
in ways that are eternally significant.*

CHAPTER 6

CALLED BY WHOM, AND FOR WHAT?

YOU ARE NOT HERE MERELY TO MAKE A LIVING . . . YOU ARE
HERE TO ENRICH THE WORLD, AND YOU IMPOVERISH YOURSELF
IF YOU FORGET THE ERRAND.

—WOODROW WILSON

I had finished speaking, and now it was time for questions and answers. A woman in the back left corner raised her hand and asked, "So, how do you know when you are called to your job?" All of the sudden, the room went completely silent. All side conversations stopped. People quit writing and looked up from their pads of paper. Those preparing to run to their next appointments took a break from putting all their stuff back into their briefcases. Everyone was listening.

"I mean," she continued, "is there any way to really be sure that you are doing the most fulfilling thing possible?"

This was not a church meeting. It was not a ministry retreat. It was not a Christian conference. This was a meeting in Detroit of the design engineers from around the world of one of the Big Three auto companies. Everyone, even unbelievers, have a sense that there is something specific that they ought to do with their lives, and they are deeply concerned that they not miss those destinies.

We really were not sure how to answer. How do you explain a biblical concept to such a diverse audience? Calling is a God term. It comes straight from Scripture. It is a word Jesus uses to describe the communication between Him and His followers regarding what they will do in life. To be "called" you have to know God and listen when He talks.

It is not difficult to understand why the concept of calling shows up frequently. If we were living out our callings, we would be doing exactly what we were designed to do. We would be perfectly fit for our work. Who would not want that?

When a secular business magazine, however, features a story on calling, there is a limited amount of help they can offer their readers. Calling is not about getting in touch with yourself. It is letting God touch you. I do not determine my calling by holding a personal intellectual summit. I determine my calling by listening to my God coach me through the work path He wants me to take.

TWO KINDS OF CALLING IN SCRIPTURE

Calling, at its most basic level, is the expression of a higher purpose. In the transitory swirling currents of the temporary, calling moors us to the eternal. Beyond God, we cannot be moved. Calling constantly reminds us that our lives are larger than our puny selves. In the Bible, calling is twofold: God calls each person to Himself, to salvation, and then calls that person to his or her work as part of God's divine agenda.

When the apostle Paul wrote in Romans 8:28 that each follower of Christ is "called according to his purpose," he was explaining our adoption into the family of God. We have been, quite literally, saved. We draw our life from the everlasting life of

God. But when God says to Jeremiah, "Before you were born . . . I appointed you as a prophet to the nations" (Jer. 1:5), the calling is to a *specific work assignment*. God had a job for Jeremiah to do. Scripture records many instances of God calling people to specific work: Moses, Paul, Isaiah, Nehemiah, Josiah, John the Baptist, Elisha, and Stephen, to name just a few.

Calling, then, is both general and specific. Our calling in life, in the words of Os Guinness, means that "everything we are, everything we do, and everything we have is invested with a special devotion, dynamism, and direction lived out as a response to His summons and service."[1] Calling encompasses all of what it means to be human. In the words of Mother Teresa, "Many people mistake our work for our vocation. Our vocation is the love of Jesus." She was right. Our first calling is to a relationship with Him; yet that relationship is pursued in the context of a second subsequent calling, the work that He created us to do out of our love for Him. Neglecting either calling is a mistake.

The Bible includes many verses that speak of a calling connected to our work. Most have nothing to do with a full-time Christian vocation. Most refer to God's calling somebody to the marketplace: to cut jewelry, dig ditches, build roads, nurse the sick, take notes as a scribe, play music, shepherd, rule a kingdom. God still calls us to design Web sites. To decide court cases. To deliver copy machines.

CALLING DEFINED

My (Thomas Addington's) dad is a called man. He lives as meaningful a life as anyone I know. Well into retirement, he works tirelessly on a project that he believes God wants him to finish. This current undertaking is only the latest evidence of God's obvious call on his seventy-plus-year life.

As a young man who had just completed seminary, he and

Mom were convinced that they belonged in missions. When the mission organization told him that they really needed doctors, he promptly enrolled in medical school.

He arrived in Hong Kong in 1960 as a young physician to open an outpatient clinic. Because of the unmanageable influx of refugees from China, the Hong Kong Medical Department urged him to build an inpatient hospital. Evangel Hospital was dedicated in 1965 and, to this day, provides excellent medical care regardless of a patient's ability to pay.

When it became clear that a surgeon was needed at the hospital and none was available, Dad completed a residency in general surgery. Later in his career, when he returned to the United States, he practiced as a surgeon with the same sense of calling as the chief of surgery and chief of staff at a large hospital in St. Paul.

The road of Dr. Gordon Addington's calling has not been straight. He did not stay with the same career all his life. His assignments included different geographies at different ends of the globe. He worked in Christ-centered and secular contexts. Over his life, his paychecks came at various times from a parachurch ministry, a church, a mission organization, a private surgical practice, and from a hospital. He fulfilled job descriptions as pastor, surgeon, and organizational leader. He has degrees in civil engineering, divinity, theology, and medicine. The list could go on. It would only emphasize and confirm what people who know my dad say about him: he is a man deeply aware of his calling. Though his career had twists and turns, he never lost a clear sense of his calling.

What is Scripture's definition of calling? What does it mean to be called? Calling is:

> God's personal invitation
> for me to work on *His* agenda,

using the talents I have been given
in ways that are eternally significant.

To be called means I know that what I am doing is what God wants me to do. God calls every one of us to a specific work assignment at any given time. When Paul was speaking to philosophers in Athens, he made it clear that God had a very precise plan for individual lives: "From one man he made every nation of men, that they should inhabit the whole earth; and *he determined the times set for them and the exact places where they should live*" (Acts 17:26, emphasis added). God designed *me* to do something for *Him*.

We are men and women who do consulting, banking, truck driving, plumbing, doctoring, full-time parenting, teaching, pastoring, and a host of other things. God calls individuals to all kinds of careers. The common factor that we all share, however, is the One who has called us all.

Anchored in eternal reality, we are freed to view our work from a perspective above the constant changing of day-to-day business. At the same time, we are not "above it all," exempted from or unchallenged by the ever-changing realities of the work world before us, temporary as that work may be. God throws us in to join the fray. We plant eternal seeds in the ground of the everyday. Our work involves the implementation of God's agenda in history.

When we come to grips with the idea and magnitude of God's calling, we are less tempted to define success as a promotion to the seventeenth floor or a vacation in the Swiss Alps. In our work we are called to higher, more attainable realities and to a deeper fulfillment and sustaining significance.

CAREER VERSUS CALLING

Our word *career* comes from two ancient French roots for "cart" and "circle." The word picture is of an individual pushing a cart endlessly in a circle: the treadmill of life. Calling is not treadmill living. Calling is a picture of linear movement. It is both a summoning, a coming to, and then a commissioning, being sent on an errand. The picture here is *not* the circular, never-ending rat race, but the outward-pointing arrow of meaningful direction. The difference between career and calling is the difference between mission and activity. Calling is being released to be exactly who I am supposed to be, to do precisely what I am supposed to do for God, an assignment with eternal worth.

As long as I have doubts about my calling, I will wonder if I am doing what I am supposed to be doing. My spouse will hear me constantly making comments like "I don't know, there just is something missing at work," or "I keep wondering if I should look into some other job possibilities," or "I wonder what else there is out there that might fit me better," or "I can't wait to retire so that I can . . . ," or "I wish I could be more content with my work situation." If I don't know my calling, my work life will lack satisfaction.

Even more important, if I do not live out my calling, I compromise my ability to contribute to God's larger purpose with my work life and career. When the apostle Paul says, "David . . . served God's purpose in his own generation" (Acts 13:36), it is clear that God had a well-defined purpose for David's life work.

DIFFERENCES BETWEEN PURPOSE, CALLING, AND MEANING

The biblical concept of calling is confusing if we do not understand the difference and connection between calling, purpose, and meaning. They are not the same thing, but they are closely connected.

1. PURPOSE

Purpose in Scripture is synonymous with God's sovereign design, His overarching view of history. It is what He is accomplishing. Very few men in the Bible knew exactly what His purpose was during their lifetimes. Some of the prophets did, at least to some extent. We know God's purpose only if He chooses to reveal it to us.

My work is not some arbitrary choice that does not make any difference. Its primary objective is not only to put food on the table and provide a comfortable retirement. To be sure, the bills must be paid, but there has to be more to work than survival. My individual, personal, just-for-me work calling is part of God's larger agenda in history. I actually have a part in God's plan.

We are to serve God's purpose, whatever it is, even though we do not necessarily know all the details. Here is what we do know:

- God operates off of a master plan, even though He does not always tell us what it is.
- God specifically fits each of us as Christians into the larger workings of His overall plan.
- We serve His purpose through faith by following our best understanding of His calling on our lives.

As Christians, we know our work has purpose because we are serving a God whose purpose is bigger than us. To look up into the night sky at the end of the day and know that our work and life are part of His bigger plan supplies an inner joy and satisfaction that can come from nothing else.

2. CALLING

If purpose is something I have to serve, calling is something I need to discern. Calling is what I do individually to fit into God's purpose. Because I am "called according to His purpose," it is imperative that I discover exactly what my calling is. According to Ephesians, "In him we were also chosen [or called], having been pre-destined according to the plan of him who works out everything in conformity with the purpose of his will" (1:11). God calls us to serve in a way that is consistent with how He has designed us. Finding my calling is about learning how God has designed me to serve Him.

3. MEANING

God's purpose is something I serve. My calling is something I know. Meaning is something I am to enjoy. If I am accurately liv-ing out my calling, I will experience the incredible sense of mean-ing from my work that only God can provide. Meaning is a fruit. It is the peace and satisfaction of knowing that my work is in con-cert with God's plans.

King Solomon was one of the wisest and wealthiest men of all time. He was a very successful monarch with a special gift from God in the realm of wisdom. He wrote the Old Testament book of Ecclesiastes near the end of his life. He devoted portions of it on different topics, like wisdom, pleasure, and knowledge. One entire part is devoted to work. In that section Solomon hammered at the theme that godly people will find meaning, satisfaction, and fulfillment in their work:

> A man can do nothing better than to eat and drink and find satisfaction in his work. This too, I see, is from the hand of God, for without him, who can eat or find enjoyment? (2:24–25)

> I know that there is nothing better for men than to be happy and do good while they live. That every man may eat and drink, and find satisfaction in all his toil—this is the gift of God. (3:12–13)

So I saw that there is nothing better for a man than to enjoy his work, because that is his lot. (3:22)

Then I realized that it is good and proper for a man to eat and drink, and to find satisfaction in his toilsome labor under the sun during the few days of life God has given him—for this is his lot. (5:18)

Who receives the gift of work-related meaning? Everyone? Negative. Only those who are godly:

To the man who pleases him, God gives wisdom, knowledge and happiness, but to the sinner he gives the task of gathering and storing up wealth to hand it over to the one who pleases God. (2:26)

If I do not have a personal relationship with God, then my career does not have nearly the sense of meaning that is available to a Christian. I may be single-minded and mission driven in what I do, but my work is necessarily a task force of one. It is all about me. I do the same work, but I do not receive the same enjoyment, the same meaning, the same satisfaction, because I am on my own errand. I lack the meaning of my work's being part of something larger than myself. Only Christians can serve God's purpose, know God's calling, and experience God's gift of meaning. We are to serve purpose. We are to know calling. We are to enjoy meaning. All three are work-specific and God-specific.

WHAT CALLING IS NOT

We need to be careful here. Work is not the sum total of our lives, nor was it ever meant to be. We must never hide behind our callings as an excuse for our work to own us in inappropriate ways. In our personal experience and from our conversations with hundreds of people over the years, there are at least three common traps that we need to run from:

1. Allowing work to drive me

There is a big difference between one who is driven and one who is called. Among other things, driven workers often allow the demands of the job to set the agenda for their lives. *I am busy because I can't help it; the job demands it,* so the thinking goes. As work heats up, the company grows, promotions come, the number of customers increase, and the phone rings more often, I have no choice but to run faster, devote more hours, stay up later, get up earlier, and travel more often.

As one who is called, I will work very hard. To be sure, there will even be seasons when special circumstances at work will require extra energy and time. The problem is that many today live at work as a way of life. The job drives them, not the calling. The calling that I must follow, however, comes from Jesus—not my job. Unless we understand that distinction, the job that Jesus calls us to can actually end up calling us away from Him.

Drivenness emanates from internal restlessness, a never-satisfied striving, pride, and ego. Calling comes from knowing what I am supposed to do to fit into God's overarching purpose. It is Jesus who calls me. In doing so, He brings satisfaction, rest, a sense of togetherness, completeness, and wholeness. The same Jesus who calls to work also says to us, "Come to me, all you who are weary and burdened, and I will give you rest. Take my yoke upon you and learn from me, for I am gentle and humble in heart, and you will find rest for your souls. For my yoke is easy and my burden is light" (Matt.11:28–30).

2. Asking work to supply my identity

When I became a Christian, my name was recorded in the Lamb's Book of Life. Nowhere does Scripture indicate that my occupation will be recorded alongside my name. My identity comes from Christ.

How Paul saw himself before he met Jesus was directly tied to what he did as a Pharisee. His work supplied his identity. One gets the impression that the list was well rehearsed:

> Circumcised on the eighth day, of the people of Israel, of the tribe of Benjamin, a Hebrew of Hebrews; in regard to the law, a Pharisee; as for zeal, persecuting the church; as for legalistic righteousness, faultless. (Phil. 3:5–6)

But after he became a Christian, he switched his identity from his work to his Lord: "But whatever was to my profit I now consider loss for the sake of Christ . . . I want to know Christ" (vv. 7, 10). This was the secret to Paul's contentment and peace over the course of a life that experienced wildly varying swings of circumstance.

3. Using work to ignore my family

A number of years ago, I was with the founder of a major retailer as he addressed a group. In a moment of candor, the man related that members of his family were unhappy with all the time he was spending growing the company. He kept promising his wife, "Just one more store." Finally, his wife quit asking and he stopped promising, because both of them knew he was going to continue regardless.

We no longer have any excuse for not giving our families a balanced portion of our time and attention. Promise Keepers, as a movement, has addressed more men on that topic than anyone else. In addition, authors like Gary Smalley, Wellington Boone, John Trent, James Dobson, Dennis Rainey, and Steve Farrar give us tremendous help in knowing how to be good husbands and fathers.

A calling to work does not take away from our privileges, obligations, joys, and pleasures of home life. If, over time, our work ends up stealing from the family, we have misunderstood how calling at work intersects with life at home. It is not either/or but both/and. As we mentioned in chapter five, our callings to work and family are not mutually exclusive. Both are equally part of God's plan for our lives, and we are called to balance in both arenas.

THREE CHANNELS FOR GOD'S CALL

I have never met anyone who is uninterested in knowing what they are supposed to be doing. Everyone—those who follow Jesus as well as those who do not—have an increasingly insatiable desire to pursue a career that fits who they are.

The question then is, how do I know what God is calling me to do? God seems to convey His call on our lives through means that fall roughly into three general categories:

1. By name
2. By placing a desire in my heart
3. By arranging a clear path

These are the topics of the next three chapters.

Scripture is so incredibly helpful and practical on so many levels: "useful for teaching, rebuking, correcting and training in right-eousness" (2 Tim. 3:16). We often turn to the teaching portions of the Bible as we move forward in our walk with Jesus. But the nar-rative portions, which are sometimes overlooked, provide rich examples of how God has built relationships with His people through history. It is to those narratives of the Old and New Testaments that we turn next in our exploration of how God calls.

CHAPTER 7

CALLED BY NAME

IT IS MEN WHO WAIT TO BE SELECTED, AND NOT THOSE WHO
SEEK, FROM WHOM WE MAY EXPECT THE MOST EFFICIENT
SERVICE.

—ULYSSES S. GRANT

The man was just doing his job. Someone had to, and he was intensely task focused in his work. His job description probably read something like, "Stop the threat. Thwart the competition." It was the kind of dirty work that you reserved for a rising star who was earning his stripes. It was an honor to be asked. One thing was for sure: if he succeeded, it was the kind of high-profile assignment that would place him on the fast track.

In his profession, title and position meant everything. This was not the kind of organization where everyone's office was the same size and whoever arrived first in the morning could park close to the front door. Rank has its privileges.

To be a Pharisee was itself an accomplishment that automatically conferred societal status. These Ph.D.s of the Scripture were disciplined, learned, and pious. They functioned as scholarly interpreters of the Law contained in the Hebrew Scriptures. Pharisees ruled the road, literally. In their Jewish culture, people stepped aside on the sidewalk and allowed them to pass unhindered. Pharisees, as everyone knew, did many good works and were therefore favored by God.

Saul was a member of this elite. What is more, he was a protégé of one of its most revered sages, Gamaliel. He was set apart even among the "set apart." His peers watched his ascending career in secret admiration and jealousy.

No one had been overly surprised when Saul was chosen to head the new task force against the new threat labeled "Christian." Although such a plum opportunity of prosecuting heretics would normally have been given to a Pharisee with more tenure, Saul was so far in front of the rest of the crowd that no one doubted he deserved the honor.

Besides, his peers were curious how he would handle this paramilitary errand. Some had even placed quiet bets on his chance of success, considering that what he was being asked to be was closer to "bouncer" than to "scholar." After all, Saul might be smart, but he was also scrawny.

Going from town to town and using a network of synagogue informants, he systematically pounded on their doors and dragged them out to accountability. They were frightened, and many were poor and unschooled. These people honestly believed that Jesus was the Son of God. He was just on his way to the next town—in this case, Damascus—and the next group of heretics. For the time being, this was his job 24/7, and he would not rest until it was finished. Acts 9 picks up the story:

> As he neared Damascus on his journey, suddenly a light from heaven flashed around him. He fell to the ground and heard a voice say to him, "Saul, Saul, why do you persecute me?"

"Who are you, Lord?" Saul asked.

"I am Jesus, whom you are persecuting," he replied. "Now get up and go into the city, and you will be told what you must do."

The men traveling with Saul stood there speechless; they heard the sound but did not see anyone. Saul got up from the ground, but when he opened his eyes he could see nothing. So they led him by the hand into Damascus. (vv. 3–8)

In an instant Saul's life was changed. He made a 180-degree about-face. He went from murderous persecutor to believer. How could that be? What happened? The answer was simple. It was Jesus, the person he had been trying to silence and snuff out.

For Paul the calling to faith and to a career task came from Jesus simultaneously. He began a new life and he never looked back.

"CAN YOU HEAR ME NOW?"

Cell phones—how did we ever live without them? Yet they can be so irritating. They cut you off in midsentence. Their static makes you—a grown and otherwise mature adult—yell to be heard. Surveys show that consumer complaints are higher with cellular service than almost any other business sector. Verizon Wireless tried to tap this frustration with its infamous "Can you hear me now?" commercial. In an ongoing series of spots, the Verizon guy is seen walking around America, constantly testing his cell phone reception. Verizon wants you to believe that they are better than anyone else at making sure you can hear who is calling, no matter where you are.

God wants us to hear our calling without interference.

How do we know our callings? The most obvious thing that comes to mind is exactly what "call" implies: hearing God talking to me directly, telling me what I am supposed to do. It might be an audible voice. It may be a dream, a portent, or a vision of some kind. Whatever it is, I have been personally visited and spoken to by God. The message He gave me is unambiguous. God called me by name. He communicated in person.

Indeed, that is one of the ways that Scripture shows calling can happen. These events are often quite dramatic, as for Samuel, who was trying to sleep in the temple when he heard God calling his name, or Mary, who was visited by an angel and informed that her calling was to be mother to the King of kings.

Of the ways that God chooses to call men and women to career tasks in Scripture, He chooses to call by name less frequently than by the other three methods. Nevertheless, call by name He does.

A BUSH THAT BURNS AND TALKS

You might say that prior to encountering a bush that talked, Moses was "downwardly mobile" in his career. After forty years in Pharaoh's household, he threw it all away. In a fit of impulsive rage, he killed an Egyptian taskmaster who was whipping one of Moses' fellow Jews. Wanted for murder, Moses fled into the wilderness to hide. He ended up in a backwater desert called Midian. There he married into a nomadic family of sheepherders.

Moses went to work for his new father-in-law as a shepherd. He had traded the palace for a tent, comfort for calluses. For the second forty years of his life, Moses walked the desert, with absolutely no inkling that he would one day go back to defy Pharaoh and lead his people to freedom.

Then, one day in his eightieth year, he came across a bush that was on fire. Moses noticed it because its flames never even charred the wood. Exodus 3:2–10 records this event. When the bush began to talk, needless to say, it had Moses' undivided attention. There was God in flames of the bush, calling his name. "Moses! Moses!"

And Moses said, "Here I am."

"Don't come any closer. Take off your sandals, for the place where you are standing is holy ground. I am the God of your father, the God of Abraham, Isaac, and Jacob."

At this point Moses hid his face, because he was afraid to look at God.

> The LORD said, "I have indeed seen the misery of my people in Egypt. I have heard them crying . . . I am concerned about their suffering . . . So now, go. I am sending you to Pharaoh to bring my people the Israelites out of Egypt." (vv. 7–10)

God was calling Moses by name to lead the nation of Israel out of Egypt. Moses could not ignore it. He could not pretend that what he was hearing and seeing was really something else. When God calls by name, it is very difficult to ignore.

IT MIGHT BE CALLING BY NAME IF . . . I HEAR GOD SPEAK

A couple of weeks ago, I was sitting across the table from my friend Mark, pastor of a large church in Los Angeles. Mark related that his father, who died when Mark was five, was both a businessman and a pastor. He was a powerful communicator of the gospel, but because of financial constraints, he held down another job even while leading a church.

Mark's mother became the sole breadwinner for the young family when his father died suddenly. Life was hard, and there was very little money. Nonetheless, Mark and his family saw God work in unmistakable ways, which seem even more incredible in hindsight than they did at the time.

When Mark was twelve, he went to a tent meeting. While there, he was compelled by a force he could not describe to go up to the altar during the invitation. He began to weep, which was not his nature. Very unexpectedly he heard God speak and clearly tell him that his life-career was to be a pastor. No one else heard the communication, but its reality is still seared in the man's memory to this day.

From that day forward, Mark faithfully pursued his God-given call to be a pastor. He did not look back; nor did he have second thoughts. His movement has only been forward toward that finish line. He planted a vibrant fellowship in the city limits of Los Angeles eighteen years ago and plans to die there helping it continue to grow.

When you encounter someone who has been called by name, there is usually no "career unsettledness" about him. He knows what he is supposed to be doing and refers to the certainty of his call constantly in conversation and in personal reflection.

IT MIGHT BE CALLING BY NAME IF . . . GOD'S SPEAKING IS CONFIRMED BY OTHER MEANS

When God calls you by name, it is seldom an isolated incident with no other indication of His tasking. Jesus came to visit Mary, the mother of Jesus, through an angel, but then confirmed that life work in subsequent conversation with Joseph. Gideon was called by God to a specific task and experienced confirmation through the famous fleece. Moses was stunned by the burning bush, but then was handed that miracle-working staff that confirmed countless times over the next decades that God's call was indeed real.

When God speaks to me in some personal and discernible way, it is a singular moment in time. Even as sure as that might make me of what He wishes for me to do, He almost always follows up with additional indications of His original message.

It's Probably Not Calling by Name If . . .
What I Have Heard God Speak Before Turns
Out Not to Be So

"God told me . . ." is not uncommon to hear in some circles of Christ followers. Yet often it turns out over time that either God was wrong or what the person heard was something besides God. With all of the heroes of the faith in Scripture, God did quite a bit of talking. Moses, for example, had extended conversations with God on a number of occasions. When he came down from a mountain and said, "God told me . . ." very few in the crowd doubted the truth of the statement.

The experience Moses had, however, is very rare. Apart from the days when the Son of God walked the earth, He generally does not choose to be in regular, audible, personal contact—at least not if the New Testament record is any indication. He communicates with us all the time in many different ways, but He seldom speaks actual words into our ears. That is not to say that He cannot do that if He wishes; of course, He can.

If I think I have heard God speak, but I have claimed that in the past and what I thought I heard turned out to be wrong, there is a very good possibility that He might not be speaking to me now in that way either. It is very important to remember that such communication is almost always reserved for unique and special—even singular—occasions. It is a huge deal to receive such communication from God, and a huge deal to claim such. We do not want to claim to have heard God speak only to be proven wrong.

It's Probably Not Calling by Name If . . .
I Can't Clearly Identify the Time or Place
of Communication

On one thing all who hear from God are unanimous: they know what He said and when He said it. Just as with Moses, there is always a time and place associated with the experience of God's call:

With Gideon:

> The angel of the LORD came and sat down under the oak in Ophrah that belonged to Joash the Abiezrite, where his son Gideon was threshing wheat in a winepress to keep it from the Midianites. When the angel of the LORD appeared to Gideon, he said, "The LORD is with you, mighty warrior."
>
> "But sir," Gideon replied, "if the LORD is with us, why has all this happened to us? Where are all his wonders that our fathers told us about when they said, 'Did not the LORD bring us up out of Egypt?' But now the LORD has abandoned us and put us into the hand of Midian."
>
> The LORD turned to him and said, "Go in the strength you have and save Israel out of Midian's hand. Am I not sending you?" (Judg. 6:11–14)

With Mary:

> In the sixth month, God sent the angel Gabriel to Nazareth, a town in Galilee, to a virgin pledged to be married to a man named Joseph, a descendant of David. The virgin's name was Mary. The angel went to her and said, "Greetings, you who are highly favored! The Lord is with you."
>
> Mary was greatly troubled at his words and wondered what kind of greeting this might be. But the angel said to her, "Do not be afraid, Mary, you have found favor with God. You will be with child and give birth to a son, and you are to give him the name Jesus. He will be great and will be called the Son of the Most High. The Lord God will give him the throne of his father David, and he will reign over the house of Jacob forever; his kingdom will never end."

"How will this be," Mary asked the angel, "since I am a virgin?"

The angel answered, "The Holy Spirit will come upon you, and the power of the Most High will overshadow you. So the holy one to be born will be called the Son of God. Even Elizabeth your relative is going to have a child in her old age, and she who was said to be barren is in her sixth month. For nothing is impossible with God."

"I am the Lord's servant," Mary answered. "May it be to me as you have said." Then the angel left her. (Luke 1:26–38)

More examples could be used, but the pattern is obvious. When God calls someone by name and you ask him or her to relate the experience to you, that person can do so in living and moving color. People remember. It is not fuzzy. If I think God has called me by name and I cannot recall the time or place, then I probably was not called as I thought I was.

"WHO MAY I SAY IS CALLING?"

I have a brother-in-law who likes to phone up at work and pretend he is a client. He always feigns an accent and rants and raves, making a ridiculous complaint about our service. My secretary rarely catches the joke and passes the call on to me as legit. Each time he varies his vocal disguise to try to throw me, but I know his voice. There is no doubt who is on the other end of the line. Even though it is a dead give-away, he never fails to make me laugh. When God calls us directly by name, there is no doubt about who we are listening to. It is such a rare event that it usually marks the rest of a person's life. When God calls in this way, we had better pick up the phone and listen.

CHAPTER 8

CALLED BY DESIRE

THE BEST CAREER ADVICE TO GIVE TO THE YOUNG IS "FIND OUT WHAT YOU LIKE DOING BEST AND GET SOMEONE TO PAY YOU FOR DOING IT."

—KATHERINE WHITEHORN

To this day there is a controversy over who first reached the North Pole: Robert Peary or Frederick Cook. Although solid proof seems absent, one fact is certain: their explorations more than ninety years ago provide a case study in human motivation.

Without question, Peary was obsessed. He often claimed himself a victim of "arctic fever," an unaccountable and driving urge to stand on a particular spot of polar ice, the earth's northernmost point. For more than a quarter of a century, over four different expeditions, Peary jealously stockpiled the necessary inventory of technology, strategy, money, material, and resources to stake a flag—as well as his name—on the North Pole. In his quest he was fierce, indomitable, creative, single-minded, and often ruthless.

In contrast, Dr. Frederick Cook's interest in the North Pole was periodic and seemed to be largely fueled as a foil: he disliked

Peary. Peary had hired Cook as a surgeon and anthropologist for his first expedition in 1891. Ten years later, at his own expense, Cook was part of a relief expedition to treat Peary and his team after another failed attempt. Peary, in poor health, was not a gracious loser; his ill temper offended Cook.

In 1907, Peary planned yet another attempt and began to calculate meticulously what it would take to reach the North Pole: clothes, sleeping quarters, advance teams, dogs, and methods of supply. He would leave nothing to chance; his plans were precise and flawless, the result of twenty-five years of firsthand knowledge.

Cook was not as thorough. Hearing of Peary's plan, Cook and a wealthy friend quickly put together an expedition of their own, launched in August 1907. Peary, unaware of Cook's attempt, set off on February 19, 1908.

On April 2, 1909, Peary, his partner, and four Eskimos made the final assault toward the North Pole: five days of grueling, nearly nonstop, sleepless march. On April 7, he stood on the ice that he believed to be the North Pole.

Upon his hoped-to-be-triumphant return to New York, Peary was greeted with news: Cook's claim, just five days earlier, that he had reached the Pole less than a year earlier—on April 21, 1908. Having gone off course on his return trip from the Pole, Cook and his crew were forced to winter in an ancient dugout on James Sound, living off the land to survive, thus delaying the news.

Although Cook's claim was generally dismissed as fraudulent, he had accomplished at least part of his objective: to steal the thunder from Peary. A controversy, fanned by rival newspapers supporting each of the explorer's claims, raged for the next five years. After pursuing his obsession to be the first to reach the North Pole for nearly half of his life, Peary never fully received recognition for his effort.

ANATOMY OF DESIRE

What looks like obsession from the outside is sometimes nothing less than the insatiable desire behind a calling. There is something that compels, drives, and pushes. It cannot be ignored or brushed aside. As the novelist Leo Rosten reflected about his own profession, "The only reason for being a professional writer is that you can't help it." A calling is something that you cannot help but do. The requirement to go or be or do comes from a mysterious inner coercion that is invisible and often misunderstood—both by the individual who lives with it and those who watch it.

To be "called by desire" is like having an internal gyroscope. Even if you lean the other direction, its centrifugal force pulls you back toward its preferred axis. This type of inner compulsion drives you and is not a matter of choice. Denis Diderot, the famous French encyclopedist, was right on the money when he observed that "only passions, great passions, can elevate the soul to great things." Such desire is a God-given propulsion. Its sense of calling can be difficult to live with—and without. How do you explain a force that is often neither logical nor observable? But then again, how could you go on without it?

THE AGITATION OF FEELING CALLED

Nehemiah felt such a burning within his being. Like his predecessor, Daniel, Nehemiah was an extraordinarily gifted chief executive who served the most powerful ruler of his day. Artaxerxes I was king of the Persian empire in the midfifth century BC. As his official cupbearer, Nehemiah had direct access and great influence. The cupbearer also held power as the keeper of the royal signet ring and acted as the chief financial officer of the kingdom.

Needless to say, Nehemiah was in the know at the highest level. He was a statesman, a sophisticated and seasoned veteran of palace politics and intrigue. He was wealthy and well positioned. The man was a keeper of state secrets. He was intimately familiar with behind-the-scenes dealing and maneuvering at court.

Bad news was part of the currency of Nehemiah's job—especially since the Persian empire was in turmoil during his tenure. Even with all that experience and exposure, when this man of authority had a casual conversation with his brother, he fell apart—literally. In Nehemiah's own words:

> Hanani, one of my brothers, came from Judah with some other men, and I questioned them about the Jewish remnant that survived the exile, and also about Jerusalem. They said to me, "Those who survived the exile and are back in the province are in great trouble and disgrace. The wall of Jerusalem is broken down, and its gates have been burned with fire." When I heard these things, I sat down and wept. (Neh. 1:2–4)

A new variable rocked Nehemiah's world. His status quo was shattered by news from his homeland that tore at his heartstrings.

What Nehemiah heard troubled him deeply. The walls around Jerusalem lay in rubble. Nehemiah wept. He mourned. He cried some more. For over four months he fasted and prayed. This was no "here today, gone tomorrow" burden. Nehemiah was affected to the core of his being. Ultimately, that depth of feeling became evident even to the king. The nineteenth-century French writer Honore de Balzac observed about such a calling: "Vocations which we wanted to pursue, but didn't, bleed, like colors, on the whole of our existence." Try as he might, Nehemiah could not hide his overcome heart from the keenly observant king for long.

He had every reason to put on his game face. You never wanted to offend a Persian king. They did not retain their right to the throne by kissing babies and making campaign promises. They were known for their capricious ruthlessness. Over the forty years of Artaxerxes' reign, he put down at least two rebellious challenges to his power. Such kings had to constantly question the faces around them, looking for any sign of discontent or crack of disloyalty.

Those at court were expected to enter his presence with nothing less than a countenance of joy. After all, who would not be thrilled to stand in his presence? Nehemiah, however, could not hide his heavy heart. For months after he was given the truth of the sorry state in Jerusalem with its devastated walls, he descended into such heartache that he could no longer hide his anguish from the king. Nehemiah's heart must have skipped a beat when the king one day asked what was the matter. Luckily, by then Nehemiah had a firm sense of his calling and did not let even the potential threat of a king's wrath stand in the way of pursuing his mission:

> In the month of Nisan in the twentieth year of King Artaxerxes, when wine was brought for him, I took the wine and gave it to the king. I had not been sad in his presence before; so the king asked me, "Why does your face look so sad when you are not ill? This can be nothing but sadness of heart."
>
> I was very much afraid, but I said to the king, "May the king live forever! Why should my face not look sad when the city where my fathers are buried lies in ruins, and its gates have been destroyed by fire?"
>
> The king said to me, "What is it you want?"
>
> Then I prayed to the God of heaven, and I answered the king, "If it pleases the king and if your servant has found favor in his sight, let him send me to the city in Judah where my fathers are buried so that I can rebuild it."

Then the king, with the queen sitting beside him, asked me, "How long will your journey take, and when will you get back?" It pleased the king to send me. (Neh. 2:1–6)

There was no other explanation to Artaxerxes' reaction than that it was a God thing. The burden that Nehemiah felt was God's undeniable call to a very specific task of rebuilding the wall.

CALLED TO RETAIL

When you talk with Tami Heim, it is obvious that she loves retail. She recently retired as president of Borders, Inc., which gave her responsibility for both Borders Online—a joint effort between Borders and Amazon—and the 480 superstores in the United States that are the core of the company. How did Tami arrive at the place where she led an enterprise of 19,000 employees, $2.4 billion in revenue, and millions of customers? She was called by desire.

Desire is not something that you pick, like ordering off a menu. It picks you. It often arrives at a young age. Tami describes how the desire of her internal gyroscope led her from early on all the way through her career. She explains:

> I always knew that I wanted to be in retail. At a very early age I was intrigued by the department store environment. I had family that had worked in retail. My mother was a salesperson, and even when there weren't a lot of women in the workplace, she used to sell vacuum cleaners. So there's a little bit of that genetically in me; but I knew that that's what I wanted to do.
>
> I was strongly encouraged by someone in the business to "get a job and make sure this is what you want to do, because

retail is not for everybody, and you're either going to absolutely love it or you'll want no part of it." I needed that counsel.

When I turned sixteen, Lazarus, a division of Federated Department Stores, was opening a new store in Indianapolis. So I went marching right in to get an application, because this is where I was going to work. And it was so funny, because I'd never done anything like this. And the woman kept saying, "We aren't hiring any more part-time people." Well, I didn't even know what "part-time people" were—I was sixteen years old. And I just kept sitting there and she kept coming out, and she said, "We're not hiring any part-time people," and I said, "Well, I'm not really sure what kind of people you're hiring, but I really want to work here, and I've waited a very long time, and I've filled out my application, and I would just love the opportunity to talk to someone." So she took me in to meet with the Human Resource manager. We had a great conversation, and I walked away with the job.

And that was really the beginning. I absolutely loved the experience. We were opening a new store, and I had the opportunity to work in all the departments. I loved it. I was so eager to do as I had been directed. I went through sales training and I worked very hard on the floor to make sure that I was following my cycle of selling and that I was treating customers the way that they wanted. And I believe that was recognized by people within the organization. Even though I was in high school, they gave me a lot of additional responsibility. By then I was totally hooked . . .

In college, Tami continued to follow her desire. She chose Purdue University specifically because of its Retail Institute. She continued her successful career at Lazarus/Federated, where she remained for twenty-two years before moving to Borders, eventually reaching the president's office. Tami, like Nehemiah, was agitated by a feeling. Desire is almost always found at the core of a calling.

PARADIGM OF FOCUS

When you encounter someone who is called by desire, you generally meet a very focused individual. She knows what she is about, and she is tenacious about getting there. Sidney Madwed advised, "If you want to be truly successful invest in yourself to get the knowledge you need to find your unique factor. When you find it and focus on it and persevere your success will blossom." A calling requires self-examination. You cannot know your calling if you do not first know yourself. Calling is a process of definition, identifying both what you are and what you are not. To determine if a desire is not just a bad case of heartburn, but instead a genuine, God-given direction, here are some questions—both positive and negative—to use as filters:

It Might Be Calling by Desire If . . . the Sense of Urgency Is Persistent and Relatively Longstanding

A calling is more than a passing fancy. Life always has zigs and zags. We are not talking here about a "passion of the moment": two months ago your overwhelming urge was to open a retail business in the center of Chicago, and today it is to become a professional athlete. No, a calling is not your latest case of goose pimples. It is an abiding passion of your soul. When God places a desire on your heart and then uses that desire to call you to do something specific, it is usually something that builds and is seasoned over time, not something that just shows up on your doorstep today for you to do tomorrow.

One of our good friends, Andy Murray, illustrates that reality. For as long as we have known him—roughly fifteen years—he has been interested in consumer branding: how it works and how it can be used to sell product. There are, of course, thousands of individuals in business interested in the same thing. Andy, however, was convinced that he had a different angle than others. He worked first at Procter & Gamble in branding, then at DaySpring Cards. Although he was able to accomplish some of what he wanted to, he became convinced that in order to really maximize his idea, he would need to begin his own company.

He did just that, calling his business BrandWorks. His specialty was not the usual territory of media advertising, like TV, but in how branding actually sold stuff on the shelf in retail environments. His passion, as he puts it, was to "turn shoppers into buyers." He was so successful that his firm was bought out by Saatchi & Saatchi, one of the world's leading advertising firms. This new division, called Saatchi & Saatchi X, is the thought leader in this new frontier of positioning products at the retail level to sell at a greater rate and volume than their competing brands sitting next to them on the retail shelf.

The largest manufacturing, retail, and marketing companies are now racing to figure out the new approach to shelf brand positioning that Andy developed. Andy's calling began with an idea that would not go away. It was a burr under Andy's saddle. Eventually it seemed substantial enough to launch out as an entrepreneur with just one employee and an intern. At each stage God confirmed his calling. Now Andy is CEO of a global company. He began with a unique and persistent idea that would not go away. When he articulated his thinking near the beginning of this pilgrimage, what he heard back from people was, "What are you talking about?" Now it's "How do you do that?"

Andy feels, without ambiguity, that he was called to pursue this idea. It did not come to him in a flash, but instead built over time. The longer he thought about it over the years, the more clear it became to him that it was an idea worth trying. If a desire is from God, its sense of urgency will be persistent and enduring.

It Is Probably Not Calling by Desire If . . . I Am Completely Unequipped to Get the Job Done

God equips whom He calls and calls whom He equips. If I feel called to do something that is outside the bounds of who God has made me, then it probably is not a calling after all.

Calling is more about doing than it is about thinking. Calling requires that I take action that results in accomplishing something. It is not primarily about ideas that I just roll through my mind. Many people have dreams that they equate with God's call; but calling is about doing, not dreaming. Dreaming is often part of the equation, but the dream must result in tangible motion.

Early in my parents' marriage, they chose to pursue a career in missions. That had always been a dream of my mother's as she was growing up. As part of the process for preparing to become missionaries, they met with the governing board of the mission they were hoping to enter. During that interviewing process my parents asked the board what kind of missionaries they needed most. As it turned out, they needed medical personnel, specifically physicians.

After my dad left the meeting, he did not dream about being a doctor; he promptly applied for medical school. Following graduation, he gathered his young family and went to Hong Kong, where he built a hospital and spent a major portion of his career.

J. K. Rowling *had* a dream to write a book. In that regard, she is not particularly unique. One day she sat down at a keyboard and began to write. The difference is that she had what it takes to do it, and she sat down and did it. Of her own journey, she said,

"It does not do to dwell on dreams and forget to live." A calling is not something you just dream; it is something you must be capable of bringing to fruition.

IT IS PROBABLY NOT CALLING BY DESIRE IF . . . I QUIT WHEN I ENCOUNTER SIGNIFICANT HURDLES

There is a tomb I visit as often as I can. It is located in Macau, until recently a Portuguese colony off the coast of China. During my growing-up years we vacationed there as a family while living in Hong Kong. My dad always took us to the old Protestant cemetery when we were on holiday.

It is as much a garden as a graveyard. Over the entrance door is a plaque identifying it as the cemetery of the Protestant church of the English East India Company. It was founded in 1814. If you walk in past the chapel and then continue to the bottom of the ramp, you come to the tomb of Robert Morrison.

Robert Morrison was the first Protestant missionary in China. At age twenty-five he arrived in 1807, filled with a driving passion to see the Chinese people come to know Jesus. He died twenty-seven years later a very discouraged man. Over his entire career he had only baptized ten Chinese. He considered his work a failure. Yet his influence continues to this day, as he made perhaps the most significant contribution of any single person to the Christian church in China. Why? Because Robert Morrison translated the Bible into Chinese. He also compiled a six-volume Chinese dictionary. It was he who made possible the huge influx of missionaries that followed, including Hudson Taylor, the founder of China Inland Mission, one of the greatest interdenominational faith mission initiatives in history. Tens of millions of Chinese have come to know Christ as a direct result of Morrison's lifelong effort.

His tomb is simple. It reads in part, "Robert Morrison, 1782–1834. The first Protestant missionary to China, who after a service of 27 years cheerfully spent in extending the Kingdom of the Blessed Redeemer, during which period he compiled and published a dictionary of the Chinese language, and for several years labored alone on the Chinese version of the Holy Scriptures . . ."

How hard was it for Morrison to fulfill what was obviously a "calling by desire"? First, his mother made him promise that he would not leave his native Scotland as long as she was alive, he did not leave until she died. Then, to actually travel to China, he was forced to go by way of the United States, which was nowhere near the most direct route. Why? Because the English East India Company, which controlled all travel between England and China, refused passage to missionaries. They were afraid that the evangelizing of Chinese would hurt business. Finally he arrived in Canton and went to work. What was that like? Listen to this description by William Milne, the first assistant who joined him: "To acquire the Chinese [language] is a work for men with bodies of brass, lungs of steel, heads of oak, hands of spring steel, eyes of eagles, hearts of apostles, memories of angels, and lives of Methuselah." Life is seldom a cakewalk for one who hears God call by desire. A calling is tenacious. It works itself out despite the obstacles. The Chinese Bible is testament to Robert Morrison's persistent pursuit of his calling against all odds.

DESIRE TO THE END

Like Arctic discoverer Robert Peary, Ernest Shackleton was another early twentieth-century polar explorer with a calling. Shackleton, however, is known not for his success and discovery, but for the epic story of his perseverance in the face of failure and almost-certain death. In 1914 Shackleton set out from England with twenty-six men to become the first to cross the continent of Antarctica by foot.

Shackleton's calling was driven by desire. His father was a doctor who pushed his son to enter medicine, but Ernest felt his heart drawn to the ocean. On his first voyage, when he rounded Cape Horn, off the southern tip of Chile, he found himself looking over the rail to the south. He felt lured to the Antarctic. The dream of probing the globe's icy underbelly captivated him. He was agitated by explorer's wanderlust. At that point no one had ever been to the earth's southernmost point before.

You do not reach the South Pole in a day. Like any calling, it is a lifetime pursuit. For twenty-four years Shackleton worked at his calling, slowly climbing the maritime ranks in British merchant shipping. His was a desire followed by action and preparation.

His 1914 Antarctic expedition was actually his third. He was not discouraged by failure, nor by the fact that in the meantime, someone had already reached the South Pole ahead of him. Undeterred, he redefined his objective. He would lead an expedition that would be the first to cross this forbidding, uninhabited continent on foot. Calling always finds an opportunity for expressing itself.

One day, before Shackleton was to land his men on Antarctica, their ship became hopelessly locked in by an earlier-than-usual ice pack. Their ship was finally crushed by the ice. The ship sank, and the voyagers found themselves involuntary castaways on a frozen island destined to melt from underneath them. Shackleton realized that his primary calling now was not to traverse a continent, but to captain an expedition of men, come what may.

The story of their long subsequent ordeal is so impossibly grueling as to defy belief. They pushed, pulled, and sledged three lifeboats over six hundred miles of contorted ice. Finally, fifteen months after being marooned on the ice, they reached open water in April 1916. They then sailed north one hundred miles to reach the nearest land, Elephant Island.

Realizing that the island offered them little hope of rescue and not much more than a sliver of terra firma on which to die, Shackleton chose five other men and set out in one of the boats to get help from the nearest human settlement, South Georgia Island. Shackleton was gambling his own life on extremely bad odds to go for their one chance to cheat death. It was an eight-hundred-mile voyage across the earth's worst ocean in an open boat. They had to rely on readings from a sextant in a thrashing boat to plot their way. If they misnavigated by even one degree, they would miss the tiny speck of land and sail into frozen oblivion.

Their eighteen-day voyage to South Georgia is considered one of history's greatest feats of seamanship. But landfall did not bring rescue. They found themselves wind-bound on the uninhabited side of South Georgia. They would have to cross the snow-covered, mountainous arctic island on foot. With frostbitten hands and feet, ninety feet of rope, and a carpenter's pick, they made a thirty-six hour climb that has only been accomplished one other time—just a couple of years ago by elite British commandos outfitted with full modern alpine gear. Finally, on the afternoon of May 20, 1916, they walked into the island's whaling port from which they had originally departed for Antarctica. When they opened the door of the whaling headquarters, the director asked the ghosts of men standing before him, "Who the heck are you?" One of the unrecognizable skeletons staring at him replied, "My name is Shackleton."

Against all odds, Shackleton fulfilled his calling. He did not lose one single man. All survived and were rescued, thanks to his leadership. The name of his original ship proved prescient of his expedition's fate. It was the *Endurance.* How did Shackleton persist to success? He was just following the deep desire of his innate and lifelong calling to lead.

CHAPTER 9

CALLED BY A PATH

A MAN PLANS HIS STEPS, BUT GOD DIRECTS HIS PATH.

—SOLOMON

King Edward VIII brought Great Britain to the edge of a constitutional crisis. He ascended to the English throne in January 1936 as a bachelor, but during his first year of reign, he decided to marry Mrs. Wallis Simpson, a newly divorced American woman he had met in 1930 while she was still married. Edward had no desire to leave the throne, but the Church of England would not accept their monarch marrying a divorcee.

Edward would have to choose between the woman he loved and the crown. After a reign of just 325 days, Edward abdicated the throne on December 10, 1936, by signing this two-sentence declaration:

I, Edward the Eighth, of Great Britain, Ireland, and the British Dominion beyond the Seas, King, Emperor of India, do hereby declare my irrevocable determination to renounce the Throne for Myself and for my descendants, and my desire that effect should be given to this Instrument of Abdication immediately.

In token whereof I have hereunto set my hand this tenth day of December, nineteen hundred and thirty six, in the presence of the witnesses whose signatures are subscribed.

Edward R.I.
Signed at Fort Belvedere in the
presence of Albert Henry George

With those simple words, King Edward VIII walked away from his job. He later married Simpson and died in exile in Paris in 1972.

Edward's startling choice abruptly changed the British line of royal succession. His brother Albert immediately became king in his stead. Albert's daughter Elizabeth would not be the queen of England today if it had not been for Edward's abdication. Elizabeth experienced how external events sometimes define the path of your calling. Yet each of us, like Edward, must decide whether to accept that mantle or walk away from it.

OBVIOUS CALLING

Quality specialist Philip Crosby has said, "The great discoveries are usually obvious." Sometimes calling is self-evident. It is not a question of what your calling is, but if you want to accept it. Edward was going to be king, unless he chose to walk away. There is no evidence in Scripture that Josiah spent restless nights wondering what he was supposed to do in life. When the time was right, someone took him by the hand and led him into the throne room. When he walked out to all the pomp and circumstance, he had a crown on his head.

One of the ways God calls is by making things so certain that though the individual might wrestle with *if* he wants to do it, he will not wrestle with *what* he is supposed to do. Sometimes it is a golden opportunity that falls in your lap or an extraordinary ability that you were born with. Other times it is an option that has God's fingerprints all over it. Family-held businesses, for example, often create an expectation that a child or grandchild will succeed the previous generation. You know what you are to do; now you just have to come to terms with the sacrifice it will mean for you.

Mike and Karen were making campus visits to their short list of potential graduate schools. They had made reconnaissance trips from Mississippi where they lived to programs in Colorado, Florida, Texas, and finally, Boston.

They left for Boston with reservations, because it is a long cultural leap from Mississippi to Massachusetts They toured the quaint New England campus. It had research resources that could potentially be a treasure trove for Mike's work. They met with several potential professors. Two seemed especially good fits for what Mike wanted to do. One laid out a path showing how he could mentor Mike to the next step and pointed to a list of previous students whom he had successfully launched on their way. As they flew home to Mississippi, Karen did not say a word. She just cried. The reason was that the choice was obvious, and she knew the cost. Now they just had to come to terms with the reality of a move from the Deep South to the Yankee heart of the North. Eight years later, the degree from Boston was in their rearview mirror, and they were well down the road that it had opened up before them. Neither one looked back with regret. The choice had been obvious. The sacrifice had proven well worth it.

CALLED TO SAVE A GENERATION

Such gates of obvious calling are usually covered with risk, overwhelming fear, and intimidation on the front side, but almost always prove painted with unusual opportunity and gratification on the other. Esther provides another case in point of such a calling by the path of life arranged before her. The year 539 BC was a banner year for the battered Jews in Babylonian exile. The prophets predicted that they would return home after seventy years. That is a long time to wait to see if a theory is true, but God did His work right on schedule.

When Cyrus of Persia defeated Babylon, he instituted a new policy: deported peoples could return to their native lands. Although Cyrus intended this as a shrewd way to extend his empire, the effect was that the Jews were free to return to their homeland.

This new deal, however, was not necessarily such a great bargain. Seventy years was a long time: homes, businesses, and family networks had been established in Babylon. There was not much to move back to anyway. The capital city of Jerusalem was in ruins. The land had long been ravaged, scavenged, and neglected. It took a hardy frontier mentality to leave it all behind and start over. Consequently, not all Jews accepted Cyrus's offer. Only fifty thousand attempted the risky return to Judah. About half a million stayed in Babylonia, Persia, Egypt, and other places where they had settled. A beautiful young woman named Esther was one whose extended family chose to remain behind.

Esther was an orphan and was raised by her cousin Mordecai, a Jew who held office in the palace household of the Persian king at Shushan. Mordecai had parented well, and Esther had responded accordingly. One commentator describes her as a "woman of deep piety, faith, courage, patriotism, and caution, combined with resolution; a dutiful daughter to her adopted father . . . There must have been a singular grace and charm in her aspect and manners, since she obtained favor in the sight of all that looked upon her" (Esther 2:15).[1]

Mordecai served the Persian king Ahasuerus, the third successor after Cyrus. According to the historian Herodotus, Ahasuerus was bold, ambitious, handsome, stately, and self-indulgent, not to mention vicious and violent. He killed his own brother, his nephews, and was said to have beheaded the builders of a bridge because flooding and storms destroyed it. When his first wife displeased him, he divorced her. When he declared a countrywide search for a replacement, it was not a position with much job security. Nonetheless, Mordecai allowed Esther to enter the running in the consort contest. She won the king's heart and ended up with the job.

As with all courts of kings and queens, the palace of Ahasuerus was full of politics and intrigue. Its drama was not a game but was deadly serious business. If you played the game and won, there were great rewards. Those who lost often ended up dead.

Haman was one of those "players" who hover around centers of power, constantly positioning and fawning for any scraps that might get thrown their way. He was a master of political intrigue. In truth, however, like many two-bit politicos, he was not much more than a common thug dressed in the uniform of the king's entourage. He hated the Jews and designed a plan to exterminate them from the kingdom.

Haman was unaware, however, that Esther—now the queen—was Jewish. Hearing of Haman's plot, Mordecai warned Esther, "Do not think that because you are in the king's house you alone of all the Jews will escape. For if you remain silent at this time, relief and deliverance for the Jews will arise from another place, but you and your father's family will perish. And who knows but that you have come to royal position for such a time as this?" (Esther 4:13–14).

Esther swung into skillfully choreographed action. Risking her own life, she approached the king and foiled Haman's plan, thus condemning him to the gallows. Esther and Mordecai were the heroes of the hour. Every Jew in the country owed their very lives to their compatriot queen.

Unlike Josiah and Edward, Esther's calling was not based on her last name. Her heritage was common, not royal. God, nevertheless, supernaturally arranged her path in an undeniable way. Becoming queen was the clear and obvious path that God had designed. It is from her story that we get that famous phrase "for such a time as this." Like Esther, you have been called by God to fulfill his work for you "for such a time as this."

SIGNS ON AN ARRANGED PATH

How can I discern if the path I am on is indeed arranged by God? How do I make sure I am not chasing a rabbit trail? Might it be an errand of my own making? As you prayerfully try to discern if you are being called by a God-ordained path, here are several trail markers to look for:

IT MIGHT BE CALLING BY ARRANGED PATH IF . . . THE OBJECTIONS YOU FACE IN YOUR DECISION ARE NOT NEGATIVE CONSEQUENCES IF YOU DO IT, BUT ARE IF YOU DON'T

The calling of an obviously arranged path does not allow much space for choice, equivocation, or ambiguity. It just seems clear-cut—at least to most of those looking on. That does not mean that decisions do not have to be made. It just requires different kinds of choices. It is not a choice about *what* to do, but *whether* to do it. Its inherent inertia can only be changed by a choice to *not* act, rather than the other way around. If, for example, you feel called to launch out as an entrepreneur and start a new company, it is very possible—even probable—that the response from friends and family will move along the lines of:

- "Oh, really?"
- "You aren't honestly thinking of that, are you? Are you serious?"
- "Who else knows about this? What do they think?"
- "What if it doesn't work? Then what?"
- "What makes you think you will be good at this?"

Think, in contrast, what people must have thought about Edward not remaining king:

- "What is he thinking????"
- "How can he walk away from that kind of honor and privilege?"
- "He was born for this!!"
- "How dare he think he can just up and leave!"

It Might Be Calling by Arranged Path If . . . What Everyone Else Expects Makes Logical Sense to Me Too

Just because everyone else expects someone to fill a specific role is not enough by itself to qualify as God's call on his or her life. Calling is God's person-specific invitation. In the end the individual being called must finally determine if the call is for him or her. I will stand before Jesus one day and give an account of my life, and it will not be good enough to say, "Everyone expected me to do it, and I never really thought much about it myself." Calling is something I answer to Jesus for, so whatever others think must be confirmed in my own spirit.

As we work with individuals who are thinking through those issues, there are many occasions in which they feel confident that this is the position they have been created to fill. They love the business, have the right skill set, have been educated to do the job, and have gone about getting the practical experience necessary to take over. Then there are others who wrestle with the decision. Apart from the opportunity and expectation, they probably would not choose this mantle of responsibility. They might prefer to do something different or would at least like to explore that possibility.

I sat down with a friend recently at a restaurant owned by the successful company that his father began. To take the business to the next level will require a number of years of focused commitment on the part of the person growing the company. Frankly, the son would much rather do something else completely. As a result, his relationship with his father is strained.

The son's decision will necessitate a major shift in the thinking of the family that owns the company and might even result in an ownership change. The son feels strongly that he and his family are at a season of life intersection that includes a separation from the family business. Even though everyone is looking at him for leadership, it does not make sense to him. Whether or not such an arranged path is a true calling is a decision that only the individual can make. As W. Somerset Maugham observed, "Tradition is a guide and not a jailer."[2]

It's Probably Not Calling by Arranged Path If . . . I Have the Wrong Last Name

We use the idea of the right or wrong last name somewhat loosely: we don't really mean that, for God to arrange your path, a particular last name is a prerequisite. The fact remains that many of the examples in Scripture and elsewhere illustrate that this type of calling *are* "last name" kinds of situations.

Some callings have critical credentials. If you don't have them, you are usually safe to consider yourself *not called.* It is just not in the cards.

We work in many family-held companies where last names mean a great deal. This is a principle that many hirelings in family-held companies would do well to heed. Every once in a while we have what to us seems like a bizarre scenario that moves along the following lines: an individual occupies a key role in a business controlled by a family. Indeed this person is often so important to the proper functioning of the company that in any other organizational context he would be a natural candidate for the top job. He has the education and the performance to back it up. It is clear he adds value to the enterprise. He is loyal. He may even be a confidant to the owner of the business. He is frequently called on to represent the company when the owner is unable to do so. He honestly thinks that he will someday run the business. Except . . . Except what? Except that the owner has a child. When the key individual walks out of the room, the owner expresses his or her true desires, a succession plan that almost always involves the child with the right last name.

Even in situations where succession is an unspoken topic, the key hired individual referred to above is often the only one in the whole company who thinks he might actually lead the company in the future. Everyone else has read the handwriting on the wall: the child with the right last name will be the one chosen.

This category of calling, where a specific path is arranged by God, refers to situations where the one being called often must have qualifications for the job that extend beyond simply being at the right place at the right time or having the right résumé. That is sometimes hard to understand for people in cultures with egalitarian values, like the United States, in which it is assumed that any position ought to be open to anyone who can make the case and the grade. The fact remains that factors like birth, connections, and intangible qualification are often part of the calling package.

IT'S PROBABLY NOT CALLING BY ARRANGED PATH IF . . . THE TIMING IS OUT OF SYNC

Prince Charles will someday be the king of England. When? Nobody knows. He is ready and has been for some time. He is getting older, already well into middle age. He has been called to that task since conception.

Charles will become the king of England when his mother decides it is time, or when she dies. He has very little to do with his highest calling. Until the crown is on his head, he is called to wait and to look as productive as possible in the meantime. Charles must content himself with knowing that, at least for now, he is called to be a prince. It is not yet time for him to be king.

Being patient with God's timing pays off. David went through much the same waiting game, only it was far more difficult and complicated. Saul was technically still king, but David had been anointed the true king after God rejected Saul's reign. Not only did David have to wait, but he was forced to do so as a fugitive, living in caves along with a circle of his loyal friends. Saul was exceptionally jealous of David's leadership and popularity and chased the young future ruler into hiding,

The waiting was agony for David, especially so because God had made it clear through the prophet Samuel that he—not Saul—was the rightful king. David's struggle was not trying to figure out what he was called to. He had to battle to be patient while he hung around waiting for it to happen.

Years later, after he had been delivered from Saul, King David expressed the gratitude and exhilaration he felt after God vindicated him:

He reached down from on high and took hold of me;
he drew me out of deep waters.
He rescued me from my powerful enemy,
from my foes, who were too strong for me.
They confronted me in the day of my disaster,
but the LORD was my support.
He brought me out into a spacious place;
he rescued me because he delighted in me. (2 Sam. 22:17–20)

The LORD lives! Praise be to my Rock!
Exalted be God, the Rock, my Savior!
He is the God who avenges me,
who puts the nations under me,
who sets me free from my enemies.
You exalted me above my foes;
from violent men you rescued me. (2 Sam. 22:47–49)

Because God has placed us in space and time and "determined the times set for [us] and the exact places where [we] should live" (Acts 17:26), calling always operates within the boundaries of His timing. We are not called to do something at the wrong time. If the timing is out of sync, then the calling is incomplete.

STEPPING OUT WHEN THE PATH IS CLEAR

Karol Wojtyla was a humble man. He was born in relative obscurity in Poland. He grew up as one of the millions of Europeans whose lives were engulfed by the Second World War. When his university studies were interrupted, he had to work in a quarry. When the dust finally settled and he sorted out his options as a young man, he felt increasingly called to the priesthood. He entered a secret seminary, because such training was illegal under Poland's new Soviet regime.

Wojtyla was never your stereotype of a priest. He loved acting, poetry, philosophy, and the outdoors. He was confident of God's call to the church, and ministering to youth became his passion. He was known for taking students from his parish on kayak camping trips in the Lake District and on alpine hikes in the Carpathian Mountains.

Wojtyla's path was limited, however, by historical circumstance. His options as a Catholic priest were severely restricted in a country controlled by an atheistic Communist party. The secret police did everything it could to thwart him. Wojtyla was undeterred. He kept doing what God had called him to: ministering faith to a people trying to survive in a system hostile to God. Over time he was made a bishop, then a cardinal. Wojtyla did not know it, but God had him waiting.

In August 1978, Wojtyla was urgently called to Rome. The pope had died. Getting the documents necessary for the trip to the West was a hassle. The party always made foreign travel hard, even for church officials. Finally, the needed papers came through. He scrounged what hard currency he could from friends. He would need every cent to get to Rome and would have to take his own food to eat on the train. He quickly packed an overnight bag with his meager belongings and boarded the Krakow Express.

As a prelate from the Eastern Bloc, Wojtyla attracted little attention among the college of cardinals that had been convened in the Vatican to pick the next leader of the Roman Catholic Church. He did not have an Italian last name as had every pope for the last four hundred years. Nor did he wear the Italian shoes that marked the Western life of the Vatican officials of the curia who met him at the station. No, all he had were the plain, dusty, black proletarian-style shoes that were the only thing available in

Krakow. That did not keep him, however, from walking forward, following his calling.

Wojtyla and the other cardinals locked themselves in seclusion in the Vatican chapel to pick the next successor to the bishopric of Peter. Two days later, on October 16, white smoke pillowed out of the chapel's chimney. A new pope had been chosen. It was only a little while later that the doors of the papal balcony opened and out walked Wojtyla as Pope John Paul II.

Among the great figures of the twentieth century, none perhaps is more famous for his faithfulness to the calling of the path he found before him than Pope John Paul II. He confronted Communism. He led his own people to freedom, and with them a whole continent besides. He led the Catholic Church in its resistance to secular modernism. Even unbelieving historians begrudgingly admit that he was called "for such a time as this." If Wojtyla teaches us anything, it is that sometimes the question is not which path, but whether I will *step out* when the path is clear.

CHAPTER 10

WHICH CALLING
PLAN AM I ON?

CALLING IS THE ARCHEMEDIAN POINT BY WHICH FAITH MOVES
THE WORLD.

—OS GUINNESS

The Gdansk shipyard was an ordinary place to work. This Polish industrial complex, which built huge oceangoing cargo vessels, looked no different from what you would find on the Houston shipping channel, or in Norfolk, or in the port of Los Angeles. Every morning a herd of men with hard hats and lunch boxes walked in. After eight hours of welding, grinding, painting, operating cranes, and driving forklifts, the whistle sounded and a herd of hard hats headed home.

On August 14, 1980, the whistle blew, but nobody went home. Instead, one man jumped the fence and joined all of those already inside. His name was Lech Walesa. Walesa was an electrician who had been fired for protesting the plight of workers in the face of staggering rises in food prices, instituted by Poland's then Communist government. The whole shipyard came to a standstill as all the workers joined in a sit-in strike demanding that Walesa be reinstated. Soon other factories joined in sympathy. Unrest among workers spread throughout Poland. People were demanding reforms.

Facing the specter of a swelling insurrection and the very real danger of a Soviet threat to restore order, the Marxist president of Poland asked to negotiate with the workers. They chose Walesa to represent them. As a result of these historic talks, the government agreed to allow the organization of free trade unions, and the next month Walesa helped found Solidarity, the first free trade union in the Communist world.

For the next year Solidarity thrived, spreading the dream of autonomy to every workplace in Poland. In December, however, the boot descended once again, martial law was declared, and Walesa was arrested. By 1989, however, social unrest was once again rising. To avert chaos, the Communist Party called for free elections, freed Walesa, and asked for his help. Running under Solidarity, Walesa was overwhelmingly elected president of Poland.

How does an electrician defy one of the greatest empires in the history of man? How does he go from a shipyard to the president's office? The answer is simple. He follows his calling, one step at a time. For Walesa, at first it was a vocation of choice, wiring ships. Then he was fired. Then it was a calling made clear by the appealing opportunity to represent his coworkers by negotiating for freedom. Then he was arrested. Eventually, by the time he was elected to lead a nation, it was clear that Walesa was an ordinary man following a path arranged by the great Conductor of history.

Os Guinness is right. Calling is nothing less than an invitation by God to use our work to move the world. Exhilaration comes from knowing that my current work assignment is from God and that I am uniquely designed by Him to accomplish it. In *Good to Great*,[1] author Jim Collins recommends that companies identify what they can be better at than any other organization in the world. That is the feeling that ideally should accompany the correct fit between me and the work task God has prepared for me. In the middle of the stress and sweat, the labor and tears, the ups and downs, the good and bad, the wins and losses, should come some sense that "I am made to do this!"

The reality is that calling is often very difficult to pin down. A feeling of "career unsettledness" frequently invades our peace. Often we speak with successful men and women who hold significant positions of influence who are seriously thinking about changing the direction of their careers. After the office door is closed, the conversation often begins with, "Let me tell you what I've been wrestling with . . ." They are thinking about making a transition and are torn about what to do.

Why does it have to be so hard? In theory, it should be rather straightforward. Jesus talks and, as His child, I listen. He has a task for me, and I am ready and eager to jump on it. He asks me for my all, and I want to serve Him. All the same, I still don't know what to do. I am confused. Inquiring minds want to know. Our desire to know is intense, precisely because we understand how high the stakes are in this search. Fulfillment. Meaning. Living a life of significance.

At its core, God makes calling a crucial part of our faith journey. "Being sure of what we hope for and certain of what we do not see" (Heb. 11:1) is a lifelong progression of patiently waiting on God to show Himself to us, begging Him to talk with us, making sure our lives are oriented to hear the voice of the Holy Spirit, and stepping out to do what we think He is prompting us to do.

Calling is always critical and often confusing. For some followers of Jesus, calling comes with ease, and they exude confidence about what they are about. For most believers, however, settling on their calling is a complex and mysterious process. It requires constant attention through all the seasons of their lives.

CALLING ASSIGNMENTS CHANGE

It would certainly be easier on everyone if, once we found our calling, we could count on that being what we do for the rest of our lives; but that is often not the case. Your calling to any one job or career may be short-term. Jesus worked as a carpenter before He assumed His three-year public ministry. Nehemiah went from COO to a complex project manager; his assignment to rebuild the wall lasted fifty-two days. Amos was a shepherd who became a prophet. David went from shepherd to king. The key to managing twists and turns of calling is to follow the advice of FDR: "We do our best that we know how at the moment, and if it doesn't turn out, we modify it."

Whether long- or short-term, calling comes fused with purpose. It is just that sometimes, for the life of you, you just can't see it.

STEPPING INTO GOD'S LABORATORY

Whether we are uncertain about our calling and therefore searching, or certain of our calling and therefore celebrating, Colossians 3:17 is our work code: "And whatever you do, whether in word or deed, do it all in the name of the Lord Jesus, giving thanks to God the Father through him."

Calling is God's laboratory. In His laboratory, He seeks growth, maturity, productivity, and worship. Because calling involves all of who we are, the process is never supposed to turn static. Calling involves movement and change, the "pressing forward to the high call of God in Christ Jesus" (Phil. 3:14, paraphrased). Calling is key to God's purpose and our passion as the president, the pastor, or the plumber.

Richard Bolles, author of *What Color Is Your Parachute?*, tells the story of how calling was evidenced by a woman who worked as a checker at a grocery store. Describes Bolles:

> She worked in the days when there were cash registers rather than bar code readers, and she would get a rhythm going on the keys of the cash register when she was ringing stuff up. Then she would challenge herself on how she packed the paper bag with groceries. She gave recipes to shoppers who weren't sure how to cook what they were buying. She kept candy for kids and, with permission from a parent, would give it out. She did the work of a checker, which 10,000 people can do, but she did it in her own unique way. She performed all these different roles under the guise of "just" being a checker. That's a basic way a calling gets or should get traced out: Taking mundane tasks and figuring out how to transfigure them. The story in the Gospels of Jesus going up on the mount and being transfigured before the disciples is to me a picture of what calling is all about. Taking the mundane, offering it to God, and asking Him to transfigure it. It isn't a matter of doing a great work like bringing peace into the world, necessarily; it may well mean being a checker. It's in the sense that there's a uniqueness to the way in which you do the task.[2]

In the eyes of heaven, what matters is not so much the kind of work that you do, but its quality.

OBSTACLES TO TAKING THE CALL

In the process of helping folks work through what they think God is asking them to do next, a number of common roadblocks stand in the way of taking the leap and making the change:

I Don't Want to Let Go of My Financial Security Blanket

Many folks get right to the edge of taking the plunge, but step back and remain where they are because the step seems too scary. It would take too much work. Retooling and going a different direction can include the burning of lots of calories. It takes a new burst of energy and may eat into such valuable assets as evenings, weekends, leisure time, and savings accounts. One may have to earn a new degree, get additional certification, learn how to incorporate a new business, or figure out how to smoothly transition from working in a secular context to a ministry environment. Impediment, however, is no excuse for inaction, for as John F. Kennedy observed, "There are risks and costs to a program of action. But they are far less than the long-range risks and costs of comfortable inaction."

The extra investment of time, energy, and dollars can be difficult to offer up, because we like to keep the benefits we have gained. The issue of calling fits into the cost-benefit framework. If one is confident that God is calling elsewhere, then there is tremendous cost in not going there and a huge benefit to be gained by obeying that still, small voice. "Don't play for safety," Hugh Walpole warned. "It's the most dangerous thing in the world."

I Don't Know How to Get There from Here

One of the most simple obstacles is the most significant. Even after there are green lights regarding all other questions, perhaps the most common stumbling block is figuring out how to get there. Entering unfamiliar territory requires a road map, and many do not have one. In fact, high-powered career professionals who are normally skilled in figuring things out are stumped with this challenge. Their normal network of contacts does not have relevance to this question, and their usual sources of information prove unhelpful.

CRACKING THE CALLING CODE

There is no silver bullet in solving the calling question. That lack of easy and immediate solution does not mean, however, that we cannot figure calling out. In fact, we know Jesus wants us to hear His voice, so how do we move forward? Let us suggest a protocol of questions to work through in coming to a conclusion and a solution.

WHAT IS THE STATE OF MY RELATIONSHIP WITH JESUS?

Everything begins and ends with this: the vitality of my walk with Christ. If I am not consistently in Scripture and on my knees in prayer, I will have little confidence that what I am thinking is what He is thinking. While we are encouraged to pray without ceasing, there are some intersections especially that require that our antennae be directed toward God, and this is one of them. We have no right to take the calling matter into our own hands, and that is precisely what we do when we begin to make career decisions *without* being in a serious God-listening mode.

Wrestling with calling may benefit from fasting, and possibly some time off in a remote location to think, journal, and listen. Getting my head in Scripture is also crucial. It can be very helpful to find and read significant devotional books as well. At bottom line, however, hearing God's call involves putting myself in a position to hear God's voice.

WHAT SPECIFIC CLUES TELL ME THAT JESUS MAY BE STEERING ME TOWARD A CAREER OR JOB CHANGE?

A change of this magnitude does not happen out of thin air. What collection of indications have you experienced, over what period of time, that give you pause about what you are currently doing with your career? Has the Lord talked to you through Scripture? Is there a recurring thought that nags and will not go away? Do you feel a growing discontent with your present state of life? Are you drawn somewhere different? If so, why?

While identifying the signs of your potential calling, think through the three ways that God actually calls, listed in the previous chapters. Which does He seem to be using in my case? We recommend that you journal as much of this pilgrimage as possible. It is good to have it down in black and white, and helpful to review it periodically. Submitting to that discipline also helps you to "size" the situation. What seems like a huge deal when lying awake at night may not feel the same way after it is written down and read in the light of day.

What Does My Circle of Advisors Say?

We cannot do a life with Jesus alone. We are built for community, and the strength of that fellowship comes into play during times of decision like this. We strongly recommend a "circle of advisors" to help give feedback. To call them that does not necessarily mean that you have to get them all in the room at the same time. One might be your spouse; another, your brother-in-law. Others may be lifelong friends/peers, and some may be mentors you trust to give godly advice.

When you go to them during this process, we recommend that you continue to supply up-to-date information that helps them give good advice. If you have been journaling, for example, it can be useful to share what you are thinking and why. Their value will not be in *giving* the answer, but instead will be evidenced through probing questions, the telling of experiences of others who have walked this path, etc.

Is My Current Career Moving Me Toward My Skill Set or Away from It?

It is possible that career unsettledness could come from an appropriate—though uncomfortable—set of challenges on the job. Scripture makes it clear that work life will not be easy; the sweat of labor will come with virtually any job we take anywhere.

In the process of listening to God's voice regarding calling, we have found it helpful to distinguish between the actual job I have and the kind of work I do. If I hold a job doing work I am good at, in an organization that is subpar, the situation is quite different from when I am being asked to do work that I am not equipped to handle. For example, Daniel was very good at the job he did as administrator for multiple kings over his lifetime. For the most part, the kings themselves were despots. This was not a fun job. God called him to work in that less-than-perfect context, yet fully prepared him to do his work with excellence.

We are often placed by God in challenging job situations as part of the work He is doing in us and as part of what He wants to do through us there. We need to be careful about assuming that He wants us to leave just because it is not much fun. Benjamin Franklin was right when he said, "All human situations have their inconveniences. We feel those of the present but neither see nor feel those of the future; and hence we often make troublesome changes without amendment, and frequently for the worse." Ask yourself, is the tension I feel just the natural pain of God growing me in my work, or is it a symptom of a bad fit? Sometimes it's time for a job change, but sometimes I am the one who needs to be changed.

GOD'S COMPENSATION PACKAGE

What more compelling reason to get up when the alarm clock sounds each morning than knowing that God has assigned your work and cares about its quality? What a sense of intrinsic motivation! A calling provides the perfect antidote to our self-serving, self-consuming view of work.

With calling comes great relief. Understanding your calling will lead to a sense of being vocationally settled. No more endless chasing after money, power, title, position, and climbing one step further up the company ladder. Instead calling embeds itself in peace, restfulness, and contentment.

Calling tells us no less than that we are doing the very work of God. What else is worth pursuing with all our passion? With a sense of calling in our day-to-day work, we are leveraged in eternity, settled in deep fulfillment.

ARE YOU GOING TO ANSWER THAT?

When the phone rings today, we have an instinctive visceral stress reaction. Telemarketers. The boss. Unhappy clients. A cancellation. Employee problems. A snafu. A special request. More often than not, calls feel like problems. We pick up the phone in irritation, look at the number, and decide if we want to answer it or let them leave a message. Maybe it is someone we will ignore altogether.

When God calls, it is not to ask more of our work, but to make something more from what we are doing. His errand is not always easy, but it is never regretted. His call is a call worth taking, worth listening to, and worth following up on. Trust me, He has your number and has been trying to reach you for some time. It's just up to you to pick up the phone.

SERVING@WORK

Serving others. It does not come naturally. We are born bent in the opposite direction. Instead of having a fine-tuned radar directed outward toward other people's needs and betterment, we are usually focused on taking care of number one, ourselves. We are skilled at arranging information, opportunities, even relationships around our self-interested grid. "What's in it for me?" is often the single criterion.

Then, along came Jesus . . . the One who cast aside what was good for Himself and acted upon what was good for us. He broke the choke hold that self-centeredness has on all of us. It still might not always come naturally, but as a person of faith, I can learn the art of focusing on someone else's interest instead of my own.

Until I learn and embrace the discovery that it is not all about me, I will never enjoy the deep fulfillment and pure goodness of helping others. When I am the constant center of the universe, my world of work will always shrink down to a boring, empty stillness.

SERVING

*is the art and act of focusing on someone else's
interest instead of your own.*

CHAPTER 11

SERVING NINE TO FIVE

IT IS NOT WHAT A MAN DOES THAT DETERMINES WHETHER HIS
WORK IS SACRED OR SECULAR, BUT WHY HE DOES IT.

—A. W. TOZER

One night, years ago, when my oldest daughter was but a child, I was putting her to bed when she locked eyes with me and asked a question that almost every kid eventually poses to his or her dad or mom. "Daddy," she said, "why do you have to get up every day and go to work? Why can't you just stay home and play all day with me?" Of course, I gave her any dad's stock answer when he does not have an answer: "Go ask your mom." No, actually I gave her my number two stock answer. I said, "Katelyn, that is such a good question. Would you let me give you the answer tomorrow night?" True, it was way past her bedtime, but I was stalling.

That evening pushed my thinking. I sat in her bed as she slept right next to me and I rehearsed every story from Scripture that I could think of that touched the world of work. The process begun that night reconfirmed my own understanding of the divine reason I get up and go to work every day.

The next night, I tucked her into bed and was ready and loaded for bear. I had cued up my prepared fatherly presentation, ready to roll out the Theology of Work. I was equipped for questions and anything else that might come up. To my surprise and disappointment, she had forgotten the question and really wanted me to move on and tell her one of my nightly stories of Bandit, the mysterious Black Squirrel.

She may be distracted with Bandit for now, but she will have to answer those questions herself one day when she is grown. What are the motivators that can pull us out of bed even on dreary, rainy mornings? Knowing that the day holds explosive pressure and demands, what pushes us through the dark door of work for one more day? In short, *why work?*

PARADISE LOST

When we think of work, we often think about how it seemed to get off to a bad start in the Garden of Eden. For many of us it has yet to get any better.

"It was her fault!"

"No, it was *his* fault!"

"No, it was the snake's fault!"

If only Adam, Eve, and that darned snake had not messed up, there would be no such thing as work. We would have no chores, no assignments, no honey-do's, no deadlines. Life would be one perpetual spring break, full of cool breezes and sleeping late, void of sweat and all the things that accompany hard work. Right? Wrong.

As we mentioned in chapter 2, many people think that work was introduced by God as a punishment for Adam's sin. The often difficult nature of work is seen to be proof positive of its curse. In other words, if man had not sinned, work would not exist. But is that really true? And what difference does it make anyway?

How one answers these questions carries tremendous implications. What we believe directly affects what we do. C. S. Lewis, the brilliant Christian apologist, wisely wrote, "Correct thinking will not make good men of bad ones; but a purely theoretical error may remove ordinary checks to evil and deprive good intentions of their natural support."[1] The person who believes work is the curse of God and the one who believes that work is a potential blessing of God will walk to their workplace with different strides, and approach their work with fundamentally different attitudes.

Genesis 1–3 provides the basis for forging a solid theology of work as something good that God ordained before the Fall and as something that will take toil and sweat to accomplish after the Fall. Work has several significant God-ordained purposes. We see at least five:

PROVISION

On the most primary level, work provides the necessities of physical life: food, drink, clothing, and shelter. Work is a God-given vehicle for meeting our needs. Any individual capable of work should do it. Whether paid or voluntary, at home or in the Oval Office, work is not an option.

The Bible, especially the Wisdom Literature and the Pauline theology, is pregnant with warnings against idleness and exhortations to live productively. (See Proverbs 6:6–11; 10:4–5; 10:26; 12:24; 12:27; 13:4; 14:23; 15:19; 18:9; 19:15; 19:24; 20:4; 20:13; 21:25–26; 24:30–34; 26:14–16; Ecclesiastes 4:5; 10:18; Isaiah 56:10; and 1 Timothy 5:13–14.) Paul is blunt and to the point: "If a man will not work, he shall not eat" (2 Thess. 3:10; see also verses 11–12). There is no biblical support for the dreamy days of retirement. Regular work should be a part of my routine till the day I die. It might slow down or be redefined, but without work, rest will never totally make sense.

Our friend Josh had his first summer job this year. He is sixteen and just recently secured his driver's license. The only thing between him and the truck he wanted was one little thing. Cash! So what did Josh do? He went to work and sweated his way toward the purchase of his own white Chevy truck.

Every morning this summer, Josh left the house to go work on a construction crew. After forty to fifty hours of sweat each week this summer, Josh brought home over four thousand dollars. While other boys slept in till noon, Josh was doing the dirty deed we call work. Why? He had a need, and work was the vehicle to *get* the vehicle. Josh is learning to work in order to meet his own needs. My guess is that Josh will be a hardworking fellow for many, many years. No father would be concerned about Josh's providing for his daughter.

Work as provision has a communal as well as individual purpose. Through the work of men and women, God intends to meet the needs of the poor and the weak. This is a consistent message throughout the Bible. Paul writes, "If anyone does not provide for his relatives, and especially for his immediate family, he has denied the faith and is worse than an unbeliever" (1 Tim. 5:8). As we provide through our labor, we image the provision of God. God is a providing God.

CHARACTER DEVELOPMENT

By his own admission, Larry was not a confident man. He struggled to find his place in the world, to define and develop his strengths, to acknowledge and compensate for his weaknesses, and to feel that what he was doing really mattered. His question, asked mostly in whispered 3:00 AM prayers, was the same as millions of others: *How can an average guy like me make an eternal difference?*

That is what drew him to "the ministry." As a youth pastor, he had the opportunity to directly impact the course of eternal reality with every conversion and subsequent spiritual development.

When Larry took a job as a medical salesman, he believed that most of his "ministry" was over. Work would pay the bills. Soon, however, Larry discovered a whole new vista—a previously unknown frontier—for displaying the character, words, and acts of God. He did so imperfectly, for sure; sometimes he even completely and miserably failed. Nonetheless, gradually and with growing confidence, Larry began to have an impact. For the first time Larry found people were being drawn to him for who he was, not for some spiritual position he got paid for. He saw there was power in being an "average" guy for God.

Larry attributes his effectiveness to "the crucible of work." His faith was on the line. As he waited in a doctor's office just before his first sales pitch, praying that God would help him pay his ever-mounting bills, he made the first of many realizations of his complete dependence on God. If he were to simply survive in the business world with its focus on the strongest, he would have to develop a whole new level of trust. His faith was not only on the line, but was hanging by a thread in a typhoon.

His temptations to fudge his character came early in his new boss's request to overstock the hospital. A barrage of "opportunities" presented themselves for compromise, manipulation, and self-pursuit: "Do this, and you'll get ahead. Go here, and you'll see what I'm talking about. Take that, and you'll have the edge." Yet Larry, firm in his desire to serve and growing in his grasp of God's view of his work, always attempted to take the high path: integrity and excellence.

When Henry Ford looked back on his journey from farm mechanic to founder of the world's largest automobile manufacturer, he reflected, "Life is a series of experiences, each one of which makes us bigger, even though it is hard to realize this. For the world was built to develop character." Like Ford, Larry was now in life's classroom, and he was growing. He has not always succeeded, but even his failures—and maybe *especially* his failures—contributed to the development of his character.

In the crucible of the business world with its amoral worship of "whatever works," Larry began to remove the moral sludge from his life. He understood in vivid terms the meaning of Peter's admonishment:

> Make every effort to add to your faith goodness; and to goodness, knowledge; and to knowledge, self-control; and to self-control, perseverance; and to perseverance, godliness; and to godliness, brotherly kindness; and to brotherly kindness, love. For if you possess these qualities in increasing measure, they will keep you from being ineffective and unproductive in your knowledge of our Lord Jesus Christ. (2 Pet. 1:5–8)

These words were no longer simply ink on paper, but essential nourishment for his soul's survival.

As Larry sought to stay true to his spiritual anchors, a curious thing happened to him. For the first time in his life, he had a sense of his own competence, one that was remarkably free of ego. In the specific calling of his job, God allowed him to exercise not only his faith, but his own unique gifts, temperament, talents, and passions. In other words, God was maturing Larry. He was no longer Larry, the average guy, but Larry, the incredibly unique and loving creation of God.

WORSHIP

Work and worship at first sound like parts of an oxymoron. We work at the office, and we worship at church. That is where we should praise God, right? A quick tour of Scripture, though, provides a surprising list of the places we are called to worship God: on the mountain, in the desert, in Hebron, at His sanctuary, on the Mount of Olives, in bed, in the Temple, on the battlefields, in the heavens, in front of gates, in Jerusalem, in Judah, in Babylon, in a manger in Bethlehem, at feasts, and at the feet of angels. In short, we should worship God wherever God happens to be. Of course, that means everywhere.

Worship can be done anywhere, because it's not a ceremony, but a posture of the heart. As Jesus put it, "Yet a time is coming and has now come when the true worshipers will worship the Father in spirit and truth, for they are the kind of worshipers the Father seeks. God is spirit, and his worshipers must worship in spirit and in truth" (John 4:23–24). Worship is a spiritual act of the heart. It has no limitations of space. Its only requirement is a proper attitude of the heart.

When the Bible talks about working as unto the Lord (Col. 3:23), it is talking about an intimate relationship based on both spirit and truth. The quest, then, is not for a public display of worship to God, but a genuine search for a relationship that comes from worshipping the Creator and Redeemer in every possible way and in every possible place.

It's not so much where we are or what we're doing as much as for whom we are doing it. Charles Swindoll hit the nail on the head, as usual, when he remarked, "We have become a generation of people who worship our work, who work at our play, and who play at our worship." Honoring God through what we do is not something that comes naturally. We must work at worshipping God in all arenas: the office, our playground, and our sanctuary.

Our work, if it is done unto the Lord, is pleasing to God and is an intimate expression of our love for Him and our desire to embrace a vertical relationship with truth and life. It goes all the way back to Genesis, where God did the work and proclaimed it good. A job well done glorifies God, regardless of whether anyone else knows about it. It is in and of itself a "service offering" back to the Creator of the world.

Nowhere, perhaps, is our call to worship God in all spheres of life more clearly given than in the poetry of the Psalms, and in particular, Psalm 63:

> O God, you are my God,
> earnestly I seek you;
> my soul thirsts for you,
> my body longs for you,
> in a dry and weary land
> where there is no water.
> I have seen you in the sanctuary
> and beheld your power and your glory.
> Because your love is better than life,
> my lips will glorify you.
> I will praise you as long as I live,
> and in your name I will lift up my hands . . .
> On my bed I remember you;
> I think of you through the watches of the night.
> Because you are my help,
> I sing in the shadow of your wings.
> My soul clings to you;
> your right hand upholds me. (vv. 1–8)

Larry's work life had taught him that kind of desperate trust and satisfaction in God. Each of us must keep growing in our thirst for God in all we do.

MODELING

Worship through our work does not always center on what we *do*. Worship can be the result of who we *are*. Worship is a reflection of God's character from our lives. The core definition of worship is to ascribe value and worth to God. Worship involves a pause on our part: we look at God and ascribe value to Him for who He is. Our lives, each a living sacrifice, can initiate an act of worship for others. They look at our lives, our God-given skills, our blessings, and ascribe value to God. We reflect Him, causing others to worship Him. As Edith Wharton noted, "There are two ways of spreading light: to be the candle or the mirror that reflects it." God is our only source of light, but we must be a mirror so that others can see Him too.

Consider the way we use the word *work*: a small child, when her toy is broken, comes to her father or mother and says, "It doesn't work." What a curious thing to say. Wouldn't "it doesn't *play*" be much more accurate? Yet nine times out of ten, the common response to brokenness, by adult or child, is to say without thinking, "It doesn't *work*." Our choice of vocabulary is profound, revealing. It springs from a deep reality of the cosmos: things are supposed to work. And by *work* we intrinsically mean *work correctly*, according to their design, function, and purpose.

Our accustomed way of working is broken. It does not work. Heart disease, alcoholism, divorce, TMJ, depression—these are just some of the symptoms of a dysfunctional work culture. The Fall produced an overwhelming sense of cosmic brokenness, releasing a terrifying chaos into the natural order of reality. Disruption, sin, and death now reign in the place previously occupied by worship. The man who seeks after God first comes to this terrible and painful realization: "My soul is broken."

It is not surprising, then, that the work of fallen man simply does not work. Blinded by selfish ambition, stripped of worship, maimed by greed and lust, stunted by sin, he resembles a tiny, crippled, naked beggar who, in the words of C. S. Lewis, is apt to mistake jumping in a mud puddle for a luxury cruise on the sea. Most of the time, he models little more than his own puny self.[2]

The good news, however, is that God is in the business of fixing broken work lives. In a very deep sense, Jesus *worked*, double entendre intended. His work involved modeling the life, character, words, and actions of God. In John 5:19, Jesus explained, "I tell you the truth, the Son can do nothing by himself; he can do only what he sees his Father doing, because whatever the Father does the Son also does." In Jesus' words reside many great realities, but not the least of which is this: when a man aligns himself with God in all that he does, then he truly and naturally models God, just as water reflects light, a river returns to the sea, and leaves whisper in the wind. The creature cannot help resembling the Creator. God makes His new creation in our work lives as we go to Him daily and moment by moment, turning our trust from ourselves to Him.

Just as Jesus learned to model God, followers of Christ must learn from the Son. "I am the vine; you are the branches," Jesus said in John 15:5. "If a man remains in me and I in him, he will bear much fruit; apart from me you can do nothing." Growing the Life@Work I was designed for means tapping into the vine. It means staying connected to God, the only sustaining life source. As we abide in Him, among those fruit He will grow in our lives will be the Life@Work quartet of evidencing His calling, displaying character, delivering skill, and serving others.

Only as we learn of the life and character of Jesus can we begin to reflect His words and deeds in our own work. Slowly, He recreates us into the people we were originally created to be: fully human, uniquely gifted, natural in worship, and tirelessly productive. Our work begins to work. As a light does in a dark place.

SERVICE TO OTHERS

One of the ways in which that warmth is felt is through our serving others. The work that God intended always involves a mind-set of service to others. In the book of Philippians, Paul exhorts followers of Christ to "do nothing out of selfish ambition or vain conceit, but in humility consider others better than yourselves. Each of you should look not only to your own interests, but also to the interests of others. Your attitude should be the same as that of Christ Jesus" (2:3–5). Our model is Christ Himself, who, in giving up the prerogatives of being God to take on human flesh, exemplified for us meekness, commitment, servanthood, humility, and obedience.

Work is designed as both grand and mysterious. We have the opportunity, through simple acts motivated by a spirit of service, to participate with God in the day-to-day spinning of His world. In this sense, the plumber, the preacher, the policeman, and the pool keeper all stand on level ground. Whether he or she unclogs drains or souls or streets or filters, each person contributes a necessary good to the world through that act.

This utilitarian component of work has nothing to do with "me and my needs." We are supposed to be part of that big "work" machine in life. Our work somehow makes the world a better place. At the end of the day, if it is all about me and my money, then we have left something out: primarily, a service to humanity. With ability comes reciprocal responsibility. As Barbara Sher has noted, "Being gifted creates obligations, which means you owe the world your best effort at the work you love. You too are a natural resource." How much even more so from a faith view of life!

Why drag yourself back to the office for another day? Because for one thing, the daily grind of work is a "service offering" to the world God created. Work can either be something that shrinks me down to an even more self-centered existence, or it can open me up to the larger world around me. Every job offers people of faith a stage to model serving. Serving in action is a performance that makes people around us want to grab front row seats and become season ticket holders of our Life@Work.

The concept of excellent service is nothing new. The New Testament did not always call it "customer service," but the notion of serving with a smile was certainly around two thousand years ago. Serving has four different New Testament words that help bring full definition to the concept of modeling serving. These words provide four dimensions to the world of serving.

Diakonos is *serving in relation to the task we are asked to do.* It means meeting the needs of others around me through my everyday jobs and activity. It denotes the giving of help to others, such as serving tables and preparing food (Luke 10:40) or collecting funds for the needy (Acts 11:29; 2 Cor. 8:4). This is actually where the church got its word for *deacon.* It is many times translated "to attend to" or "to service."

A perspective of deaconate service is fundamental to a Christian work life. Jesus used this "diakonos" concept of serving to describe His mission. He said, "The Son of Man did not come to be served, but to serve, and give his life as a ransom for many" (Matt. 20:28). Jesus was saying, "I am in the service business." Integrating our work and our faith means following His example. Not a day goes by that we do not have opportunities to perform tasks of service.

Huperetes is *serving in relation to our specific superior.* This word is the picture of an underrower, a man sitting in the bowels of a galley ship, manning an oar. He follows the cadence of the supervising coxswain. On command, he would rhythmically strain out each stroke. We serve those under whom we work. Fulfilling your place on a team in the same way Christ would means being willing to serve others on command.

Those who have rowed in college will tell you that there is nothing more fatal to losing a race than having even one rower out of sync. All of the oars must be pulling in unison. If they do not, then someone will get what is called a "crab." A crab is the butt of the oar shoved into your stomach when your blade catches the water out of rhythm. It feels like being kicked in the guts. On a team at the office, the result of someone only serving him- or herself is the same. Serving means disciplining yourself to follow the leader and work for the good of the group.

Leitourgos is *serving in relation to the broad organization.* There are two clear uses for the word. One is the idea of free volunteering, and the other is working for hire or an assignment given to someone by the state or company. For that reason it is many times translated "steward."

Every person who works with any organization finds himself a steward of resources that do not really belong to him. Regardless of whether it is a volunteer assignment or a lifetime career post, we must model serving as stewards. Fundamentally, Life@Work is an issue of Christian stewardship.

Doulos is *serving in relation to our only Master, Jesus.* As a doulos, or bond servant, I see myself as the property of Jesus. He is my only master and commander. This dimension of serving is unique for those who wear the name of Jesus. I am not a doulos of any other. That is an allegiance that is held only for my Master. Each of us must bring our work under the lordship of Christ. He must be the Master of our careers.

These four words when woven together portray serving in all its directions with all its audiences. We serve anyone connected to a task in which we are involved. We serve anyone who is above us in our work lives. We serve anyone who is connected to the organization or company for whom we work. Ultimately we all serve Jesus, the ultimate audience and customer of our Life@Work.

CHAPTER 12

IT'S NOT ABOUT ME

I DON'T KNOW WHAT YOUR DESTINY WILL BE, BUT ONE THING I
DO KNOW: THE ONLY ONES AMONG YOU WHO WILL BE HAPPY
ARE THOSE WHO HAVE SOUGHT AND FOUND HOW TO SERVE.

—ALBERT SCHWEITZER

Alfred Nobel invented dynamite. He is most famous, however, for what he did with the fortune he made from it. He put it in a trust to create a prize to recognize those individuals who have marked our globe with exceptional service to humankind. Since 1901, the Nobel Foundation, headquartered in Stockholm, Sweden, has awarded Nobel Prizes to such recipients as Albert Schweitzer, Martin Luther King Jr., and Bishop Desmond Tutu. None set out with the goal to win the Nobel Prize or to receive its worldwide fame and huge cash award. Their motivation was simply to help and serve others. The 1921 Nobel Prize winner for physics, Albert Einstein, said it best: "Only a life lived in the service to others is worth living."

Few Nobel Prize winners have captured the heart of the world more than the small, frail nun from Albania. The late Mother

Teresa won the Nobel Peace Prize in 1979 for her work among the destitute, the dying, and the orphan children in the slums of Calcutta, India. Her address told nearly all that anyone needed to know about this model of servanthood.

Address: Missionary of Charity, Nirmal, Hriday,
             Home for Dying Destitutes, 5A
             Lower Circular Road, Calcutta, India

She requested that on her tombstone be inscribed these words of Jesus from the gospel of John: "Love me as I have loved you." As Saint Augustine wrote: "There is something in humility which strangely exalts the heart." Mother Teresa was a humble servant if ever there was one, and we are all better for her life's work.

What will be said of you and me when we die? Will anyone be better off for our life's work? A friend of mine is in the process of buying a tombstone for his parents' grave. How do you sum up a life? What does it all come down to, when you only have room for a ten-word inscription on a rock? If one of those words is not *serve*, then our lives will have been tragic wastes of self-indulgence. Contrary to conventional wisdom, the bottom line of a career is not how far you advance yourself, but how far you advanced and served others.

YOUR SERVE

The word *servant* is a rich, biblical concept that conveys the idea of working for and in the direction of someone else. There are well over a thousand references to *servant, serving,* and *service* in the sixty-six books of the Bible. It is a central component of the message of Christianity. It is a quality that God emphasizes and elevates as a universal language for all who have passed beneath the cross of Christ.

It is a secret to life that the world has recognized as well. The great humanitarian and Nobel winner Albert Schweitzer observed, "I don't know what your destiny will be, but one thing I do know: the only ones among you who will be really happy are those who have sought and found how to serve." Serving has to be the core of our work or it will not have a core at all.

But what is serving at its core? When stripped to the basics, what does it mean and what does it look like?

Serving is the art and act of focusing on someone else's interest instead of your own.

That definition will demand a role reversal for most of us who live in this country and a culture where self-driven, self-deserved attention is the common currency of exchange. Chances are that you probably will never win a Nobel Peace Prize, but every act of serving has its own reward.

REDRAWING YOUR UNIVERSE

Serving others requires a Copernican revolution of sorts. Prior to 1543, even the most brilliant minds mistakenly mapped the universe as revolving around the earth—what is now known as the Ptolemaic worldview. Going against almost every shred of accepted science, tradition, and authority, the Polish astronomer Nicolaus Copernicus placed not the earth, but the sun, at the center of the universe. Once this radical heliocentric idea was proven and finally accepted, it reordered our understanding of our solar system and revolutionized astronomy.

Each individual must undergo a Copernican reordering to become a lifetime servant. We must redraw the universe around others, not ourselves. As John the Baptist said of Jesus, "He must increase, but I must decrease" (John 3:30 KJV). A heart motivated to serve requires a paradigm shift. Life is found not in self-gratification, but in meeting the needs of others. As Jesus said, "Whoever wants to save his life will lose it" (Matt. 16:25). Most of us get up every day and live to save our own lives. Work is about me. Christ-motivated service, however, reverses the equation.

Joe White, founder of the nationally known Kanakuk camps in Branson, Missouri, calls this the "I am third" philosophy. God is first, others are second, and I am always third. At Kanakuk, the highest recognition passed out each week of camp is the "I am third" award. Most offices today are dominated by the competition for the "I am first" award. How much different they would look if they were defined instead by an "I am third" philosophy.

Some time back, I remember seeing a national magazine cover article with a caption that read, "Self-Centered and Proud of It." The cover sketch that illustrated the lead article was a large, ever-expanding balloon head, loosely tied to a tiny man's shirt collar. The predominant message of our culture that is piped into all the channels of our entire existence is "What about me?" or "What's in it for me?" or "How about me?" When someone gets a promotion, we ask what that does to *our* salaries. When a new strategic plan is rolled out by management, we are concerned about *our* workload. If the company had a bad year and earnings are down, we immediately grab a calculator and refigure our bonuses.

The results of a narcissistic corporate culture are cancerous. "Certain and destructive by-products accompany a life of self centeredness," observed psychologist James Dobson. "A friend likes to say you only have one chance to be self-serving with someone. After that you have marginalized and chained yourself up. The philosophy of 'me first' has the power to blow our world to pieces, whether applied to marriage, business, or international politics." The recent decade of boardroom scandals is a direct result of the "me-ism" ethos of the 1990s.

Your work is either serving or self-serving. Most in business today are just trying to blow up their own balloons as big as possible. Christlike serving is the exact opposite. It is the art of pumping someone else up, not myself. J. B. Phillips explained the role of selfless serving in Christ's revolutionary equation of life this way: "Christ regarded the self-loving, self-regarding, self-seeking spirit as the direct antithesis of real living. His two fundamental rules for life were that 'love energy,' instead of being turned in on itself should go out first to God, and then to other people."[1]

What would our work lives look like if they were restructured upon such a foundation? One thing is for sure: our places of work would not be the same.

In the last decade, an employee-evaluation tool has worked its way through the business community. It is called a "360-degree performance audit." Basically, it is the evaluating of someone's performance based on input and feedback from all the people that surround him. Those over him. Those under him. Those next to him. Those he buys from. Those he sells to.

Suppose your company initiated a 360-degree servanthood audit? How would you fare? How would those around you score you on being interested in other people, not just yourself? Would they say that you have discovered the Copernican revolution?

ADD SERVING TO YOUR JOB DESCRIPTION

Regardless of my occupation, my title, and my authority, if I work around people, I can model serving. Serving is not a function of status, power, or station. Any and all of us can serve.

- It means getting to know people as people, not just human work machines.
- It means learning their names, their spouses' names, their parents' names, and maybe even their kids' ages and birthdays.
- It means getting involved with people, not always keeping a professional distance.
- It means becoming a good listener, not just a good talker.
- It means asking more questions and then looking people in the eyes and listening to their responses.
- It means remembering the conversation.
- It means taking the time to figure out how I can affirm someone else, get someone else promoted, get someone else's project funded, not just my own.

Any of us can do that. It is not a question of IQ, education, training, or even job experience. Serving does not even require a job interview. See a need and meet it. It is that simple.

Is serving risky? Yes, it is. People are messy. The closer you get to them, the higher your chances of getting dirty. Your service will not always be noticed or appreciated. It will often be taken for granted. It will drain you. Serving is literally spending yourself.

People hurt, people have emotions, people need direction, and people need leadership. Yet in the process we will be stretched. Investing in others, we are enriched. As Bob Moawad suggests, "Help others get ahead. You will always stand taller with someone else on your shoulders."

How do we know if we are serving others? Robert Greenleaf, in the book *On Becoming a Servant-Leader*, takes a look from the other side of serving. He suggests that we ask, "Do those being served grow as persons: do they, while being served, become healthier, wiser, freer, more autonomous, more likely themselves to become servants?"[2] Real service always grows others. Its bottom line must be measured in the lives of those around me.

A few years ago we were intentionally growing our consulting business through new hires and interns. I had been interviewing people for a few weeks when a new résumé hit my in-box. The guy was impressive. Incredible credentials. Fantastic education. Unreal achievements. Off-the-chart life experiences. The more I read, the more I wondered if there was anything not recorded on his résumé.

Then it hit me. There are always things not recorded on a résumé. For example, where would anyone be able to detect a servant's heart and a servant's spirit? That made me think a little deeper. What kind of résumé would any of us have if the only virtues and entries we could include would be the accomplishments that others around us say we have helped them attain and develop? If my résumé was based upon my ability to serve others, how attractive would I be in the workplace? How are your RBI stats? The number of our "runs batted in" is our service quotient.

"SERVING" BEST PRACTICES

Serving is so foreign to us that we hardly know what it looks like. It is one of those ideas that nobody could possibly be against, yet no one has a clue what it really means. Where could you find a case study of someone who approached business that way?

Luckily, God did not leave us to our imaginations; He rolled up His sleeves, came down on the shop floor, and said, "I'll go first. Let Me show you how it is done. Just watch Me and do what I do." Listen to these words from *The Message* that give the job-focus sheet of Jesus, the Servant of all servants: "Whoever wants to be great must become a servant. Whoever wants to be first among you must be your slave. That is what the Son of Man has done: He came to serve, not to be served—and then to give away his life in exchange for many who are held hostage" (Mark 10:43–45). Jesus' words are powerful because they were backed up by a life to match.

There are two scenes from the story of Jesus that showcase what serving others is all about. In scene one, the CEO of the universe washes the dirty feet of those under Him. Don't rush by this too quickly. This would be like Donald Trump fixing a clogged toilet in the lobby of Trump towers. Somehow I can't really get that one in my mind. It would be like Warren Buffet shining the shoes of his janitorial staff. I doubt you will ever see this in an American boardroom in my lifetime.

> Jesus knew that the Father had put him in complete charge of everything, that he came from God and was on his way back to God. So he got up from the supper table, set aside his robe, and put on an apron. Then he poured water into a basin and began to wash the feet of the disciples, drying them with his apron. When he got to Simon Peter, Peter said, "Master, *you* wash *my* feet?"
>
> Jesus answered, "You don't understand now what I'm doing, but it will be clear enough to you later."
>
> Peter persisted, "You're not going to wash my feet—ever!"
>
> Jesus said, "If I don't wash you, you can't be part of what I'm doing."
>
> "Master!" said Peter. "Not only my feet, then. Wash my hands! Wash my head!"
>
> Jesus said, "If you've had a bath in the morning, you only need your feet washed now and you're clean from head to toe. My concern, you understand, is holiness, not hygiene. So now you're clean. But not every one of you." (He knew who was betraying him. That's why he said, "Not every one of you.") After he had finished washing their feet, he took his

robe, put it back on, and went back to his place at the table.

Then he said, "Do you understand what I have done to you? You address me as 'Teacher' and 'Master,' and rightly so. That is what I am. So if I, the Master and Teacher, washed your feet, you must now wash each other's feet. I've laid down a pattern for you. What I've done, you do. I'm only pointing out the obvious. A servant is not ranked above his master; an employee doesn't give orders to the employer. If you understand what I'm telling you, act like it—and live a blessed life." (John 13:3–17, THE MESSAGE)

Jesus was entering the last fifteen to twenty hours of His life on the earth. This would be the same as a father laying in the hospital and calling his family together for a few last words of wisdom before he dies. What was the single greatest, most important lesson Jesus wanted to emphasize again with clarity on His deathbed? A quick scan of all of the Old Testament personalities? No. Was it a quick review of how to preach or perform miracles? No. It was not even a review of the high points of theology. It was a never-to-be-forgotten object lesson on serving.

Why serving? Because Jesus knew that if the believers could learn to serve each other, His message and ministry would be effectively expanded when He was gone. There would be no book of Acts without serving. There would be no explosion of followers of faith without serving. There would be no New Testament without serving. There would be no churches without serving. Christ's kingdom was built on the back of serving: *focusing on someone else's interests, not my own.*

Every person needs to be served. There were no clean feet in the days of Jesus. Wait. Let me say that again: there were *no* clean feet in the days of Jesus. Everyone who was physically able walked the dirty streets and trails in open-sandaled feet. These roads were often covered with trash and sewage. There was no sanitation. It was for good reason that people of the ancient world regarded the feet as the most ceremonially unclean part of the body. Washing someone else's feet was the widest application that the concept of serving could ever be given.

The disciples had been preoccupied with the question of who was going to be the greatest. Jesus was asking them to reorient their point of reference outward to others. Everyone gets dirty. Everyone needs a bath. Life is the same way. Everyone has needs. To meet them, the disciples would have to disrobe, take off their prerogatives, be willing to get a little dirty, and put aside their desire to be great in the kingdom of God.

Service is an action, not just an idea. Jesus did not tell them about foot washing on the flip chart or pass out notes on the steps for effective foot washing. What did He do? He stood up, disrobed, knelt down, and grabbed the stinky and dirty feet of His followers and washed them. He said, "Take notes through My behavior."

I will never forget the first time I heard Professor Howard Hendricks say it. "More is caught than taught," he thundered from the front of the classroom. No questions. We knew it was true. It was true when we were little and impressionable kids, and it is true today as adults. Case closed.

Every person can become a servant. Washing feet is a simple act that anyone can perform. It does not take strength of the arms; it takes strength of the heart. It does not take brilliance; it does take humility. There is no age minimum or restriction, no education requirements, no special lineage—just a bowl of water, a towel, and someone willing to bend the knees to care for someone else's concerns.

Knowing about serving is not the same thing as doing it. It is so interesting to me that Jesus had to say to His followers in the story, "Now that you know these things, go out and practice them yourselves." Whether prayer, faith, or serving other people's interest, I have to translate my know-how into a clean set of feet on the guy next to me. The scene in John closes with Jesus' commending His followers to go and do likewise regarding the learning experience they'd just had with foot washing. *Know-how* and *act on* are not synonyms. The great Reformer Martin Luther wrote, "The life and ministry of Jesus invites us all to join the army of serving others. It requires a refocusing of life around others. It is the duty of every Christian to be Christ to his neighbor." Foot washing is a mandatory internship for a servanthood degree from "Jesus U."

THE STANDARD FOR SERVICE

Jesus was a servant. Check. Got it. I need to be a servant. Roger. I'm with you. But what would an attitude of service look like in my shoes? A second scene takes us to the next generation of believers who drew out the implications of Jesus' example as a servant for us. In it Paul is explaining the distinguishing characteristics of his Master to a new group of believers, the Philippians:

> If you've gotten anything at all out of following Christ, if his love has made any difference in your life, if being in a community of the Spirit means anything to you, if you have a heart, if you *care*—then do me a favor: Agree with each other, love each other, be deep-spirited friends. Don't push your way to the front; don't sweet-talk your way to the top. Put yourself aside, and help others get ahead. Don't be obsessed with getting your own advantage. Forget yourselves long enough to lend a helping hand.
>
> Think of yourselves the way Christ Jesus thought of himself. He had equal status with God but didn't think so much

of himself that he had to cling to the advantages of that status no matter what. Not at all. When the time came, he set aside the privileges of deity and took on the status of a slave, became *human*! Having become human, he stayed human. It was an incredibly humbling process. He didn't claim special privileges. Instead, he lived a selfless, obedient life and then died a selfless, obedient death—and the worst kind of death at that: a crucifixion. (Phil. 2:1–8, THE MESSAGE, emphasis added)

No example of selflessness will ever be greater than what Jesus Christ did. Some of the most clearheaded insights on serving to ever be are found in this passage.

Don't clutch too tightly the things that "rightfully" belong to you (see v. 6). Technically speaking, sound theology says things do not really belong to us—they are on loan, and we are only their stewards. All things really belong to God, and we are each delegated to care for them. Practically speaking, however, we feel as if things do belong to us, so we clutch those things tightly. We hold and we hoard. We hide and we stash. We maneuver and manipulate. To unravel this death grip of selfishness, we have to pry our fingers off what we are holding on to. Giving them up means holding them with an open hand. You have to voluntarily give up your rights, your prerogatives. There is no other path to servanthood.

Take on the perspective of the one you are trying to serve (vv. 7–8). Jesus practiced the ultimate "walk in the other person's shoes for a day." The Incarnation was His taking on the cloak of humanity. When He became flesh, He took on my perspective. There is no part of my world that Jesus does not know about and understand. He knew me before I was born, and He knows me by experience. The big news, however, is that He feels every step of my pain and confusion. "Because he himself suffered when he was tempted, he is able to help those who are being tempted"

(Heb. 2:18). Jesus can relate. He has been there. He chose to go there for you and me. Serving requires walking in the shoes of those you are trying to help.

Be ready for your act of serving to be unnoticed, misunderstood, or even rejected. It happened with Jesus (Phil. 2:8), and it will happen with us. We will go the second mile to help out, and no one says thanks. As a matter of fact, many times no one even sees us go the first mile, much less the second. Serving others means I must be satisfied to live with rewards that only God hands out. It is not a public award ceremony but a private prize within our own minds and hearts. We must take the approach of Seneca: "Be silent as to services you have rendered, but speak of favors you have received."

Know that the next world, not this one, is where the serving gets rewarded (vv. 9–11). One thing bonds all those who serve together: they are moved toward a longer view of goodness. It is the pull of the next world that provides the strength and perspective to take on the good of another. A bumper sticker I saw said it all: "Come work for the Lord. The work is hard, the hours are long, and the pay is low, but the retirement benefits are out of this world."

THE ACADEMY AWARDS

Movies win awards. Brilliance wins awards. Most acts of service do not. The Oscar winner for best picture in 2002 was a movie called *A Beautiful Mind*, the true story of Princeton Professor John Nash. Nash was a brilliant mathematician whose twenty-five-page doctoral dissertation on "Non-Cooperative Game Theory" revolutionized economics. For that amazing accomplishment he was awarded a Nobel Prize in 1994.

That, however, is not the most exceptional part of the story.

You see, John Nash was schizophrenic. Much of his life was spent haunted by delusional conspiracies whose complexities only the mind of an imaginative genius could have come up with. To him, however, they were reality. The same intuition that gifted him to see the patterns of group economic activity tragically imprisoned him in a dark world of nightmares when they turned inward and saw patterns of secret messages in everything around him. Once a promising scholar on the faculty at Princeton, he became an eccentric, mentally ill recluse living homeless on its campus.

Nash would have stayed that way had it not been for the loving care of his ex-wife, Alicia. Although she had long since divorced him to bring a measure of sanity to her own life, she did not abandon Nash. Even though he was an embarrassment, she stood by him. When others had given up on him, she looked after him. When he eventually began to fight his delusions and come out of seclusion, she was there for him. She gave him a stable place to land on his feet. For years hers was a private service of love.

Back then, while quietly taking care of him in the middle of all his madness, there was no Oscar or Nobel committee on her horizon. What she faced day in and day out was the horrifying reality of caring for a man who was a danger to himself. The reward on her mind was not fame or fortune, but the hope of seeing a beautiful mind blossom once again. As Alicia Nash experienced in Oslo, Norway, at the ceremony where John—now recovered—received the Nobel Prize for economics, service had its own reward.

CHAPTER 13

EVERYDAY SAMARITAN

THERE IS THE GREAT MAN WHO MAKES EVERY MAN FEEL SMALL,
BUT THE REALLY GREAT MAN IS THE MAN WHO MAKES EVERY MAN
FEEL GREAT.

—G. K. CHESTERTON

I was tired and ready to get home. If you travel often, I do not need to tell you about long lines and overbooked flights. The late afternoon flight departing the busiest airport in the world was no exception. It was oversold, and the gate agent, turned airline auctioneer, had begun the bribing contest. "Ladies and gentlemen, somehow we have found ourselves in an overbooked situation."

It irritated me. "Somehow?" How can they be surprised at something they orchestrated? I go on a Web site that they own and maintain. I find one of their flights that they offer to the public. I plug in my data including the payment. Then I show up and they say, "Well, we sold your seat to someone else at the same time we sold it to you." If McDonald's did that with kids' Happy Meals, there would be a riot.

"We have been authorized to offer up to $50 per ticket for anyone willing to catch a later flight and give up your seat," the PA announced.

The chess game had begun. People began talking on their cell phones and getting their tickets out to analyze possibilities. Strategy huddles were forming around the gate area.

A couple of minutes later, the bidding continued. "Ladies and gentlemen, we cannot board until we reconcile this overbooked situation. We have now been authorized to offer up to $100 per seat for those travelers who have flexible travel options this evening."

Two freshman coeds flying back to college took the bait. They jumped up and folded at $100. As they walked to the counter, they were beaming as if they had just won a game show.

Everything looked as if it was going to work out. Folks began to board the flight. As we followed one after another slowly shuffling forward, tickets in hand, like cows toward a loading chute, I was reminded that you do not beat the house in Vegas, and you do not beat the gate in Atlanta.

That is when we heard them: "Hold the plane! Hold the plane!" A family of five came dashing down the terminal toward our gate. Bags in tow, they were huffing and puffing, sweating and screaming to make the flight. There really was no danger of the plane having already left. There was, however, a real and present danger that someone was already sitting in their seats. That was about to be their biggest challenge of their already eventful flight.

The husband pulled the five tickets from his pocket and slung them on the counter, all the time pleading with the agent to get his family on the flight. The agent then began what gate agents hate: the one-on-one engagement with traumatized travelers trying to get home.

The father said very firmly, "We have our tickets. We have been flying all day. Our connecting flight was late. It was not our fault.

My family is trying to get to a wedding, and we cannot miss this flight. We have been planning on this evening for months."

The gate agent tried to let them down gently. Fearing the scene that might ensue, she relented: "Uh, ladies and gentlemen, we have a situation again," she announced over the microphone. It was as if the ticker bell had rung, declaring the trading floor open again. "If you have flexible travel plans and can take a later flight, we are looking for five more seats at this time." We found ourselves back in the bidding war.

The price of a seat was now at the all-time high mark of $200, and people were coming off the plane to redeem the coupons. (Now, just stop for a second and tell me what the gal who gave her ticket up for $100 was feeling, and what do you think she was about to do?) This place was getting circus, dirt ugly. We were now moving into the options market for savvy airline ticket traders. Deals and alliances were being formed.

At the end of the first round of option trades, they were still one seat short. I made a quick call home to make sure nothing was going on that I could not miss, and then I stepped up and volunteered my seat. You would have thought I had given that family a million dollars.

Three hours later, I boarded another flight and made my way home. No big deal. I was just replenishing some of the *friendly* in the "fly the friendly skies" marquee.

The next morning at breakfast, I retold the story to my family, evoking a myriad of responses: "I would have waited for $250." "What is overbooking and how can they do that?" "Why did the family wait till the last minute to go to the wedding?" "I would trade every ticket in every time if I were you, Dad. Think how much money you could make doing that." "That was a really nice thing to do, Dad." "What are you going to do with the free ticket voucher? Can I have it?"

Jesus told a story of a stranded traveler in need of help, but His had much higher stakes. Only the Gospel writer Luke captures the story we have come to know as "The Good Samaritan." It is the story of a traveler. He was not on his way to a nearby airport, but rather simply pounding the dust from one first-century town to the next, a commonplace routine from the days of the New Testament. The parable gives a terrific snapshot of serving in action.

This particular path was the only connector between Jerusalem and Jericho. Its seventeen miles of twisting and turning dirt road through high desert had a bad reputation for its bandits. People usually only traveled in groups to ensure protection from the robbers and gangs, but you could not always find a party to travel with when you needed it. Sometimes you simply had to risk the trip and go alone.

Such was the unfortunate case for the fellow whose story Jesus related. While making his way on the road through the pass, he was attacked, robbed, and left for dead. Eventually, along came the rest of the cast, three would-be helpers. Any of the three could have stopped and helped, but only one took the time and effort to offer aid.

All three walked by need, but only one chose to take the exit of serving. Ironically, the two who just kept right on going were highly religious Jewish clerics. Even more paradoxically, the one who went out of his way to give first aid was a Samaritan, a group that Jesus' Jewish audience would have least expected to help. You see, Jews had deep enmity for Samaritans, whom they labeled "half-breeds" and religious heretics.

Jesus' use of irony always has a purpose. Faith is not about self-ascribed identity or mere declared belief, but about action, about serving our neighbors, whoever they may be. Jesus told His listeners:

> "There was once a man traveling from Jerusalem to Jericho.
> On the way he was attacked by robbers. They took his clothes,

beat him up, and went off leaving him half-dead. Luckily, a priest was on his way down the same road, but when he saw him he angled across to the other side. Then a Levite religious man showed up; he also avoided the injured man.

"A Samaritan traveling the road came on him. When he saw the man's condition, his heart went out to him. He gave him first aid, disinfecting and bandaging his wounds. Then he lifted him onto his donkey, led him to an inn, and made him comfortable. In the morning he took out two silver coins and gave them to the innkeeper, saying, 'Take good care of him. If it costs any more, put it on my bill—I'll pay you on my way back.'

"What do you think? Which of the three became a neighbor to the man attacked by robbers?"

"The one who treated him kindly," the religion scholar responded.

Jesus said, "Go and do the same." (Luke 10:30–37, THE MESSAGE)

Jesus usually had one central message that He hoped to drive deep as He spun each parable. In this one He tells us right up front. The whole story is about the question, who is my neighbor?

Jesus was challenging His audience with the way they treated all people. He wanted His followers to realize that the scope of serving goodwill to others is much broader than our favorite two or three best friends. Every day, we, too, are faced with the question, who is my neighbor? We see people needing help. A family about to be bumped. A colleague scrambling to meet a client's eleventh-hour demand. An office mate whose car will not start. A competitor in the convention booth next to me who gets sick at a trade show. A client who asks for help on something I don't get a commission on.

Who exactly qualifies as my neighbor? The implicit question is, do I have to help *them*? The answer was unmistakable in the first-century story, and it is undeniable today. My neighbor is anyone that crosses my path and who needs help that I can afford to provide. Jesus calls you and me to be "Everyday Samaritans."

There are three elements to serving other people as an Everyday Samaritan: seeing like a Samaritan, feeling like a Samaritan, and acting like a Samaritan.

SEEING LIKE AN EVERYDAY SAMARITAN

In this story all three could-be angels of assistance were confronted with the broken, beat-up man laying over in the rocks, but they did not all *see* the same thing. The first two were religious hypocrites who only saw a ceremonially unclean carcass, which, if touched, would make them ceremonially unclean as well. They had a blind spot to need that was created by their own self-styled religion. The Samaritan saw a fellow human being in trouble; he saw an opportunity to serve.

We, too, can have blind spots to those around us, passing by people we see every day, people with needs, people we could serve. It is easy to have eyes and yet not see. The power of observation is something that must be learned. It is not something that just comes naturally.

Dr. William Osler, a celebrated medical professor of the early 1900s, became famous for how he taught his students to observe. Professor Osler would take a classful of young medical students and give them one assignment to work on all day. He gave each a microscope, a specimen slide, a pen, and paper. He then instructed the students that their assignment for that day was to study and document in their journals as many observations about that microscopic specimen as they possibly could.

This was not just some quick, fifteen-minute exercise, then on to something more active and fun. Not one hour and then on to the next lecture. No, this is what they were to do for the entire day. All day the students were to stare at the slide, noting every detail they saw. It takes focus and concentration to stay bent over looking at the same thing hour after hour, ever searching for something new and fresh.

At class the next morning, Professor Osler came in and asked each of them to report on their unique findings. As everyone shared their discoveries, he listed them all on the board. When they were done, he turned around from writing and commended them for their keen insights. He then announced to the class that their next assignment was just as critical to their formation as world-class medical doctors. He promised them with a sly smile that it would be just as exciting and meaningful as yesterday's.

He handed out more paper. Today, they were to go back to their microscopes and spend yet another eight hours making even more observations from the same slide as yesterday. The students all groaned. Some years he would repeat that process for a full week of classes. His conviction was that a physician who had honed observation skills would be a better doctor.

Edward Bulwer-Lytton was convinced of the very same thing. He believed that "every man who observes vigilantly, and resolves steadfastly, grows unconsciously into genius." To be a genius in serving people, you have to learn to see with a new set of eyes.

Stop today and look around the office. Are you seeing what is really there? Do you see the single mom with bloodshot eyes from long hours struggling to make it for her kids? Do you see the manager down the hall, whose marriage is on the rocks? When you see that boss you despise, do you also see his rebellious teenager, who stymies him at home? That employee who frustrates you—did you notice the burden she carries of raising a special-needs child?

The ability to spot people around us who are in need of serving is the first step toward practicing everyday serving. Three different men traveled by the beat-up traveler. They all saw him lying there . . . but what really did each see?

PEOPLE ALL AROUND US ARE HURTING AND NEEDY

When we peer through the microscope over and over, intently scrutinizing the injured man in the story of the good Samaritan, we begin to see other people in our world who look the same way. We are each surrounded by needs just crying out to be met. General William Booth shared the passion that drove him to found the Salvation Army when he related, "While women weep, as they do now, I'll fight; while children go hungry, as they do now I'll fight; while men go to prison, in and out, in and out, as they do now, I'll fight; while there is a drunkard left, while there is a poor lost girl upon the streets, while there remains one dark soul without the light of God, I'll fight—I'll fight to the very end!" Are you fighting for the individuals where you work, or do you just pass them by in the hall?

We must sharpen our awareness of the host of the hurting and needy people all around us who are in desperate need of an Everyday Samaritan. The journey through our lives and work is treacherous at times. Their conditions vary:

PEOPLE ARE STRIPPED OF SELF-CONFIDENCE, SELF-WORTH, HOPE, FAITH, PURITY, MEANING, AND OPPORTUNITY. In some areas of life we all instinctively wear masks to one degree or another, but as John Ortberg stated so well, "Everybody is normal, until you get to know them." Your outsides will beat my insides every time. We each put up a facade that we have it "all together." Then in other areas we are as bare as the naked man on the rocky road to Jericho. In our areas of vulnerability and exposure, we need someone from the outside to stop and see our condition, without passing on by.

PEOPLE ARE BEATEN BY COMPETITION, BY FAILURE, BY PRESSURE TO PERFORM. There were literally hundreds of hidden caves and crevasses from which thieves could jump from the dark and bushwhack travelers from Jerusalem to Jericho. In today's world of Life@Work, our greatest and most frequent threats are not bodily harm. We find ourselves beaten by other thieves named competition, stress, pressure to perform, failure, overload, and the like. The outcome is the same.

PEOPLE ARE ABANDONED, LONELY, GRIPPED BY FEAR AND DOUBT. I do not know if you have ever been the first on the scene of a serious car wreck, but you never forget the look in the crash victim's eyes. It is a bewildered stare of fear and helplessness. You see the bloodied, clammy, lonely face of shock. That is how the wounded traveler must have looked to the Samaritan. Remember, this guy was left half-dead, lifeless, and hopeless. I do not think for one minute that there was a lot of pride and self-determination in the eyes of the wounded traveler. He was frightened and desperate. If you will look around corporate America, you will see many people terrified that they will lose their jobs. You will see uncertainty in their eyes, along with self-doubt and anxiety about the future. These are the eyes of need. These are opportunities to serve staring you in the face.

BLIND SPOTS TO SEEING LIKE A SAMARITAN

Too often we similarly walk blindly through our workday, passing inertly by innumerable opportunities to serve others. Why do I often miss the needs staring me in the face? What keeps me from having a clear picture of those people in my path who are in need of serving? Two stigmas blind our vantage.

I Am Too Busy

I have said this for years, still say it, and really mean it. Everyone I know is busy. We are all on the go. Modern conveniences once billed in the post–World War II consumer boom as the ticket to an easier life have in reality made our lives incredibly more complex and harried. Fast food and microwaves mean that we no longer eat as a family. Cell phones mean we have no uninterrupted private time anymore. Now the portable content of e-mails and the Web reach us wherever we are. It is no longer just information overload, but *nonstop* information overload, following you everywhere you go. I do not know about you, but I sometimes feel I need more megs on my motherboard just to handle it all.

In such a context it is particularly hard to see the living, breathing, thinking, feeling human beings around you. If they do not contact us by e-mail, chances are we will not know they are even there. A lifestyle of serving does not come native to such a frenzied existence. Nevertheless, I cannot let the hurry and pace of my particular journey of life cause me to walk blindly by the injured travelers along my path. Without some muscle of overmanagement, the business of our day will overtake us all. We need to retrain our eyes to see all the lives that we are walking right by.

I Am Nearsighted and Consumed with Me and My World

My fun-loving father-in-law has a few quips that seem to randomly spill out in conversations. When he meets someone stuck on him- or herself, he rattles off his favorite rhyme: "I am sooo cool. I am sooo grand. When I go to the movies, I hold my own hand." Well, if both hands are on me, there is no hand to extend out to others in need. That kind of mind-set will keep anyone from noticing the depth and reality of the pain people around us are carrying.

A few weeks ago, my kids and I were looking for a place to park at the mall in order to meet friends at the food court. We had already circled around twice, looping the lanes, looking for an empty spot. Suddenly I spotted someone's brake lights ahead about to pull out. I put on my blinker and waited for the driver to get clear so I could park. Then a car the size of a battleship appeared out of nowhere and took up position for a head-to-head face-off with me. It was an elderly couple. I was there first. I had the right-of-way.

As I began making my move to maneuver our car in, one of my kids said, "Dad, you can't pull in there and take that spot from that elderly couple. You have to let them park there." And we did.

My own sense of routine and self-centeredness was blinding me from a chance to be an Everyday Samaritan. The famous German Protestant Reformer Martin Luther, said, "It is the duty of every Christian to be Christ to his neighbor." Until I shift my focus to see the interests and needs of others ahead of my own interests, serving will forever be absent from my portfolio.

FEELING LIKE AN EVERYDAY SAMARITAN

Three guys walked along the same path and encountered the same scene. A priest, then a Levite, then a detested Samaritan. Two could not walk by fast enough. One stood out in that he stopped to give aid. Why did he stop?

The story as told by Jesus does not leave it to our imaginations. Jesus said it was deep sympathy that drove the heart of the Samaritan to help. One translation calls it *pity* or *compassion*. He was moved deep down in his heart with empathy and care.

It is worthwhile to distinguish the difference between the terms *sympathy* and *empathy*. Sympathy is sorrow or sadness you feel *for* someone. The key word is *for*, which carries some distancing between you and the person in pain. On the other hand, empathy is an emotion that is shared *with* someone. Here the key word is *with*, making the link between me and the other person. Empathy requires you to connect with the interior of your own life, not just a surface, shallow, frown of sympathy.

In their excellent book titled *Leadership Presence*, Belle Linda Halpern and Kathy Lubar isolate the ability to reach out in empathy as one of the four elements of effective modern leadership.[1] Someone once observed, "The greatest feats of love are performed by those who have had much practice in performing daily acts of kindness." It takes empathy to do that. Empathy, however, grows with use. As the bumper sticker says, "Practice random acts of kindness and senseless beauty."

ENEMIES OF FEELING LIKE A SAMARITAN

Empathy is not an easy flower to cultivate. There is much in our culture and current business climate that mitigates it. Empathy is a virtue that is not heralded or rewarded. It has no year-end bonus tied to it. I doubt you will hear a seminar on it. It is just not a core American value. Several factors can stunt its development in us as well.

I HAVE BEEN BURNED BY PEOPLE AND LOST MY EMPATHY FOR OTHERS

When my wife and I first married, she had recently been working in the burn and trauma floors of a Birmingham, Alabama, hospital. The scenes and smells of a burn ward are something that you never forget. The stories she told me are emblazoned on my mind to this day. Now I rarely lay aside a newspaper story of a burn victim.

One of the frequent side effects for someone who has been burned is the loss of feeling in the scarred area. The same thing happens with us relationally. Relational burns can deaden our sense of emotional touch and our empathetic feeling toward others, leaving us cold, hard, and calloused.

Skin care is the critical factor for burn patients. Salves and antibiotics work to help the skin return to good health. Empathy requires that we work to keep our human touch supple as well. The discipline to stop and really connect with people, not just talk at them, keeps that tactile faculty of empathy soft and sensitive.

I Am a Prejudiced Bigot

Have you ever felt looked down upon? We have come a long way in this area, but we still have a long way to go. There are many areas where prejudged perceptions and preferences enter into our everyday interactions and decisions. Just last night, my wife gave me an update on the daughter of a good friend who had just been cut from her sorority pledge class. No real reason was given, but clearly it was likely because she does not come from a wealthy and connected family. It might seem rather random, but it is nothing but modern prejudice and bigotry taking place.

Last week a friend asked me to interview a candidate that his firm was considering for a CEO-level position in Arkansas. The gentleman from the Northeast seemed to have an immovable prejudice against Southerners. I could not believe it. I did not know anyone like that still existed. "The mind of a bigot," said Oliver Wendell Holmes, "is like the pupil of the eye. The more light you shine on it, the more it will contract." Bigotry inevitably makes your world a smaller place.

Two religious professionals walked by a wounded neighbor. As a matter of fact, they even altered their course to "the other side" so as to eliminate any possible contact or confrontation. Religious busyness often tramples right over human need. We can avoid serving, even in the name of religion. Formalism, ritualism, and institutionalism can drive religious machinery right over hurting, needy people, all in the name of religion itself.

This last year I ran across a small entrepreneurial company in Atlanta that does an outstanding job of embracing the Everyday Samaritan from a corporate standpoint. They have built a commercial conscience or corporate empathy that requires them to treat their employees differently. Bill is the company founder and current CEO. At a time when everyone seems to be going offshore to secure manufacturing, he is convinced that the U.S. can still compete.

How? He invests in systems that have long-term value and can add to profit margins for multiple years. He is a big believer in technology and thinks that sophisticated partnering with customers is crucial. There is one more thing, however, that stands out for Bill's formula.

Last year he was the keynote speaker at an international gathering of business leaders in San Francisco. It was this last element that he gave in his talk that rocked people's world. Bill believes in helping his employees to become better people. His company budgets and spends accordingly. They make serving their employees a corporate priority.

They employ a group who predominantly do not speak English and have very shallow roots in their communities. I once asked Bill, "Why do you and your wife stay after work every Monday night and teach English to a full house of employees?" Bill's answer told it all. "How would you feel living in a country, trying to earn a living, raising a family and not be able to speak their language? Do you know how that feels? When these employees communicate better, all the parts of their existence go up."

Eric Hoffer stated that he believed "it is easier to love humanity as a whole than to love one's neighbor." There are many companies and individuals in business who give lip service to community concern these days. Actually employing such a commitment to the welfare of specific individuals is much rarer, however. Bill makes a good illustration because he is such an exception.

ACTING LIKE AN EVERYDAY SAMARITAN

We already know that only one traveler stopped and provided help. The Samaritan saw the man in need; he empathetically felt his pain and stopped to help the injured man. What did it take for the Samaritan to put feet to his feelings? More to the point, how can I practically serve others as I go through my workday?

SERVING REQUIRES DELIBERATE ACTION

Sentiments mean nothing without deeds that do something about it. Such service of others is at the heart of a life of Christian faith. John Stott, one of this age's leading Christian statesman, has observed: "Social responsibility becomes an aspect not of Christian mission only, but also of Christian conversion. It is impossible to be truly converted to God without being thereby converted to our neighbor." The straight-shooting apostle James bluntly put it this way: if you see someone cold and hungry and only say to them, "Be warm. Be filled" but yet do nothing, you are only fooling yourself. "Isn't it obvious," he wrote, "that God-talk without God-acts is outrageous nonsense?" (James 2:15–16, THE MESSAGE). Action requires intentionality.

IT TAKES INITIATIVE. The Samaritan took a relational chance. He knew he was probably hated by the Jewish victim in the road, but he took the risk anyway. He stopped and reached out his hand, not knowing what the response might be.

IT TAKES ADJUSTMENT. The Samaritan obviously was going somewhere himself. I doubt seriously his calendar called for his roaming around Jericho, looking for assault victims to help. He obviously missed his appointment and had his schedule wrecked that day. Effective serving sometimes means accepting inconvenience.

IT TAKES SACRIFICE. The Samaritan gave his time, his money, and his compassion. He obviously got his hands dirty helping clean up the stripped, beaten man. The story as told by Jesus even says that he instructed the innkeeper to keep a tab of the cost to convalesce the assaulted man and that he would take care of the entire debt.

In business we deal in goods every day, yet we often miss their moral role in meeting needs. As Saint Clement of Alexandria remarked, "Goods are called good because they can be used for good: they are instruments for good, in the hands of those who use them properly." Goods are only good when they are taken off the shelf and put into circulation to meet real needs. Serving means spending. It will cost you some goods.

DETOURS FROM ACTING LIKE A SAMARITAN

Two people walked by the body. They detoured to the other side just to avoid it. They all had their reasons. Action always meets resistance. We each have our own internal script that suggests excuses for why we would be better off to just pass on by. Doing the right thing always has a mental enemy. Our status quo does not like to be bothered. Its inertia takes several forms.

I AM TOO SET IN MY WAYS AND ROUTINE

Another way to say this is that I am stubborn and inflexible. Routines can be a good thing. They can also blind our perspective.

I have some friends who seem to never get beyond their same old circle of cronies. They have become comfortable in their little circle. They have become very ingrown and unaccepting to outsiders. You will meet few needs and do little service if you never leave your comfort zone.

Tradition can be good, but only if it gets you to where you ought to be in the future. We all have mental ruts, our comfortable, routine way of approaching life. Routine needs a wake-up call, however, if it distances and deadens us to others.

I Am Afraid to Get Involved

The Samaritan accepted the full liability to mend his friend. He told the innkeeper that any and all charges were to be held for him to reconcile upon his return. He did not overthink his situation. Nowhere does the story give us any hint that the Samaritan suddenly felt he was obligated to travel the road day and night looking for mugged and wounded victims to service. He did not quit his job and become a full-time, one-man mobile hospital outfit. He saw someone hurt, felt compassion, and responded on the spot.

Sometimes we miss life opportunities because we make them out to be more complex in our minds than they really are. Paranoia makes every person in need a grafter trying to extract nourishment from you, and every stranded traveler a serial killer. Every employee with a personal problem is not a lawsuit waiting to happen. The Samaritan saw the situation as it was. A man had been attacked and needed help. He saw one man on the side of one road, and he responded with the resources he could give.

I Am Relationally Lazy

There are many of us who are too passive in relationships. Such people always think that it is the other person's job to initiate.

They never make the first step toward other people—maybe not even the second or third step. They have become accustomed to people pursuing them, and except for selfish pursuit of powerful people, they are all but dead in their ability to initiate toward others.

Stopping to serve is incompatible with relational laziness. It is always easier to cross to the other side of the street. Yet you will never truly live if you do not daily connect with the reality of your fellow man. Initiative means asking, "How are things at home?" It means calling the person who was laid off six months ago and checking to see how his or her job search is going. It means introducing yourself to someone you see regularly, but whom you have not met.

Haddon Robinson, one of America's best preachers, likes to say that there are two kinds of people in this world: cats and dogs. A "cat," according to Robinson, is a "here I am" person. Dogs, on the other hand, live as "there you are" people. Cats arch their backs to be noticed and to get stroked. They make you come to where they are. Dogs come to you, wagging their tails, getting up into your lap, and licking you. They have no inhibitions, walking right into your world and plopping down beside you. A cat is always busy burying its own poop, while a dog will come and lick your wounds. We need more dogs at work and less cats. Which are you?

A GOLDEN EXAMPLE

Michael Phelps had just won another gold medal in a breathtaking swim race. His competition was Ian Crocker, the favored teammate who had posted the best times in the world for the 100-meter butterfly. Somehow on the last stroke Phelps surged 1/100th of a second and touched the wall for his conquest of another gold medal.

Nineteen-year-old Phelps entered the Athens games chasing Mark Spitz's record of seven medals. He could still get eight. Phelps, however, provided one of the greatest moments of the 2004 Olympics, as well as a great lesson of an Everyday Samaritan.

Immediately after the butterfly results, Phelps and Crocker sat down for a television interview. They both talked team and about how genuinely happy they were for each other. Unlike the strutting showboat egotism of some American athletes in other events, these two unpretentiously shared the glory and the limelight.

Within the hour a special announcement shocked the media. Phelps was stepping aside to allow Crocker to swim the upcoming 400-meter relay. Phelps said Crocker was better than he was. Phelps wanted the team to have its best chance to win. Even though he had every right to swim the relay, he decided to give Crocker a chance to earn his own gold medal. Indeed, when the buzzer sounded and the relay began, Phelps was in the stands, unabashedly cheering on Crocker as the U.S. team won.

Phelps's deferral to Crocker made headlines precisely because such an example of an Everyday Samaritan is so rare. Why could the media not let it go? Because the demonstration of serving produces what my friend Robert Lewis calls "irresistible influence."

Serving has an effect on people that begs their reflection and often confounds them. How irresistible is your influence lately? Perhaps by improving your serve, you could win the positive influence game.

CHARACTER@WORK

"PEOPLE OF FAITH OUGHT TO DISPLAY CHARACTER IN THEIR WORK."

Character matters.

Personality helps. Drive and focus make a difference. Passion plays a part. Education certainly makes a contribution. Connections will open doors. But don't dare go to work without character.

Don't let anyone tell you otherwise. Character counts. You can take it to the bank. If you ignore it in yourself or others, you do so at your own peril. It is a simple fact of business. Call it wisdom. Call it common sense. Or call it the gospel truth. Character is a bottom-line issue. Period.

Don't hire anyone who doesn't have proven character. Don't accept a job from a boss without character. Don't even think about partnering with anyone in business who doesn't have it. Beware of custumers or suppliers who are known to lack it. Be wary of colleagues who compromise it. Always keep your eye on the character quotient. Why?

Because character matters.

Character

*is the sum of my behaviors, public and private,
consistently arranged across the entire spectrum of my life.*

CHAPTER 14

THE ART OF ETCHING CHARACTER

THE FINEST WORKERS IN STONE ARE NOT COPPER OR STEEL
TOOLS, BUT THE GENTLE TOUCHES OF AIR AND WATER WORKING
AT THEIR LEISURE WITH A LIBERAL ALLOWANCE OF TIME.

—HENRY DAVID THOREAU

My son and I were both standing right in the middle of the U.S. Capitol Rotunda, staring straight up 180 feet in the air to the eye of the dome looming above us. The air was thick with history and a sense of bygone days.

Our young tour guide shouted over the heads of our group, her memorized lines echoing off the marble walls, "The rotunda has been the site for VIPs to lie in state for many years. The most recent was the fortieth president of the United States, Ronald Reagan. Over one hundred thousand people stood in line all day for a three-minute walk-through to pay their last respects to him."

With that she raised her hand and turned to lead us out and down the hallway for the next memorized data dump, pushing us on through our thirty-minute tour.

I thought, *That was it? The rotunda tour is over?* There was only one problem. I was not ready to go. The fresco stretched around the ceiling of the dome stared back at me as if to say, *Stay a little longer and hear these walls talk.* I needed to taste this place a little more than this canned tour was allowing.

It had only been a few weeks since the recently deceased President Reagan had been honored here. I lingered there, reflecting on the legacy of his life.

Flags were still flying half-mast out of respect for this man. Like so many, I had watched on TV his last departure from this very room, then his funeral, and finally, his last flight on *Air Force One* to be buried back in his native California.

Why did I need to pause in the middle of the rotunda? The same reason the whole country had stopped for a week of grief and reflection. We just lost a rare leader, a man of character.

Standing there, I thought of Peggy Noonan's book on Ronald Reagan, which I had just reread. The title says it all: *When Character Was King* (New York: Penguin Publishers, 2002).

Americans mourned Reagan regardless of their political persuasions, because they sensed the passing of a great man. A 2001 CNN/*USA Today*/Gallup poll found that more Americans ranked Reagan as our greatest president than even John F. Kennedy or Abraham Lincoln. One reason is that Reagan was a person of integrity.

Whether you agreed with him or not, you knew what he stood for. When he went to the Brandenburg gate in Berlin and said, "Mr. Gorbachev, tear down this wall!" his voice had moral authority. This was not just some sound bite scripted by focus group research. It was a conviction about freedom and democracy that Reagan was known for long before he ever held elected office.

That was the man who was lying in state in this room, on this very spot, just a mere week before.

Standing there, thinking about Reagan, I looked up at the ceiling of the rotunda. The inner side of the dome is a fresco called

The Apotheosis of Washington. It is a scene of Washington's ascent to heaven. It portrays Washington as the model ruler, a caesar who rules out of uncorrupted character. This theme of character continues around the outside walls of the rotunda. Encircling us as we stood in the center of the room, taking it all in, were statues of some of our most esteemed fellow Americans: Abraham Lincoln, Martin Luther King, and Susan B. Anthony.

How do you build the kind of character memorialized here? What does it look like worked out in my field of endeavor, my work-a-day reality? Surrounded by all these historical heroes, I was reminded of a comment by General H. Norman Schwarzkopf: "Leadership is a potent combination of strategy and character. But if you must be without one, be without the strategy." My son and I stopped, marked the moment, and pondered. Character. It is a rare find these days.

In the pantheon of the Bible, one of the most famous studies on character is David. Psalm 78:72 sums up David's character as "integrity of heart." David's heart was of one piece with his life. People knew what David stood for. His character spoke for itself.

The Old Testament concept of integrity is one of "wholeness" and "blamelessness." A man or woman of integrity is a "whole" person, the opposite of a two-faced hypocrite. It is someone of authenticity and transparency. A person who lives out in action what is believed in the heart and head. What you see is what you get. Don Galer defined integrity this way: it is "what we do, what we say, and what we say we do." The key is consistency between all three. My character is a composite of my life, painted for all to stand and scrutinize. It is as visible as the ninety-six-foot fresco draped across the dome of the Capitol.

THE LINES OF OUR LIVES

The word for "character" in the Bible comes from the Greek term describing an engraving instrument. The picture is of an artist who wears a groove on a metal plate by repeatedly etching the same place with a sharp tool. After repeated strokes, an image begins to take shape.

My character is forged as a set of distinctive marks that, when taken together, draw a portrait of who I really am. Everyone has character, and it can be described: bad or good, shifty or sturdy, sordid or sterling.

Behavior and character are related, but they are not the same thing. Behavior is what I do. Character is the person my behavior has made me into. Behavior is just one action. "I behaved badly in that situation." *Character is the sum of my behaviors, public and private, arranged consistently across the entire spectrum of my life.* Any behavior, duplicated and reduplicated, forms a part of my character.

Repeated patterns of behavior wear a series of grooves that form a portrait of me as a person. The lines of my behavior over time draw a picture of my character. Sometimes that portrait is compelling and attractive. In other cases it is ugly and repelling. Usually it is a combination of the two. Even great faces have warts.

A few months ago I found myself sitting in the middle of a river. Fishing waist deep in a cold moving stream is my way of unwinding. It is where I can clear the clutter of a crowded mind and heart.

There was a huge rock in the center of the river. It was a great place for a lunch break. I crawled up on it, out of the current, and stretched out like a sunbathing turtle. Running my hand across its worn surface I drank in its sun-soaked warmth.

As I looked closer, I noticed the contours of the rock. These were not features of the mineral itself, but grooves worn in it by the water. Year after year the water has poured over and around this obstacle in its path. Waves crashing into it, trying to work under it, sometimes boiling over it, always finding a way around it. Although the waves I saw passing by at that very moment made no apparent difference, in time they would leave their mark.

So it is with character. Everything we do, every thought, every choice, is a wave with ripple effects. It is easier to see their immediate effect on others than it is to see their consequence on the rock core of our own character. Yet if you will look at the contours of your life, you will clearly see the grooves shaped by the pattern of your past.

Every time we make a decision, we cut a groove. Every time we react to a crisis, we cut a groove. When we hold our tongues and practice self-control or when we let them run loose and speak our minds, we are carving our character. When we say yes or no to a reckless temptation, we are signing our names. When you stand up to peer pressure, hold the line on truth, or return kindness for cruelty, you are cutting the pattern of your character. Author Anthony Robbins was right on the mark when he said, "It is in your moments of decision that your destiny is shaped."

HOOKING UP THE HEART

The grooves of character that mark us most deeply, however, are those that are made when no one is looking. These moves of our minds and hearts tend to make the deepest ruts—for good or ill. That is why Jesus' message to His followers almost always focused on hooking up the internal attitude with the external action.

After Jesus had recruited twelve ordinary men to lay aside their current careers and follow Him for a world-changing experience, He brought them together to give them a crash course on new thinking to help them get started walking out a new faith. He took them off to a mountain for an executive retreat of sorts. One of those present recorded what happened in the gospel of Matthew, chapters five to seven, a passage that we know as the "Sermon on the Mount."

There is an unchallenged central thesis that quickly emerges. It is that Jesus wants His new followers to understand and embrace the life of inner spirituality. Six times Jesus hammers away at His one central thesis. He takes an external action like murder and ties the internal attitude of uncontrollable anger and revenge to the judgment of sin. He ties the matter of adultery to the spirit of faithfulness. Six times He asks His followers to refocus their spiritual lenses and look past the external action to the internal attitude.

If we are going to build a sound life of character, we must hook up matters of the heart.

CHARACTER ON DISPLAY

I recently was with a friend out West on a business trip. We had a little time on our hands, so we strolled the streets of the "ole part of town." As often happens in a revitalized "historic" district, we came across a local art gallery. My friend loves art, and I am incurably curious, so we wandered in. Immediately my friend made a beeline toward a group of paintings near the back wall. He said, "I would recognize this artist's work anywhere." He and his wife had been collecting this particular artist's work for some time. He said, "It is so easy to spot this guy's work, especially when it's on display."

We all paint our character on the canvases of our lives, and they hang in public for all to recognize. People parade through our lives day after day, watching who we are, constantly catching glimpses of our character. It is *on public display*. Only the naive think that character is just a private matter. It is as public as the fresco on the roof of the Capitol dome. It cannot be hidden. We may succeed in hiding certain behaviors, but our overall character always shows its colors in the end. No exceptions.

Character is like a leaky pen in your pocket. It always finds a way of bleeding through. To the extent that I have lived a life of compromise, I will eventually be exposed. If, on the other hand, I have striven for faithfulness and integrity, then someday I may need that track record to vindicate me, as a friend of mine found out when he was falsely accused.

Getting sued is never fun, nor is it particularly good for one's reputation. When the lawsuit is for sexual misconduct and you happen to be a high-profile pastor, it really is *not good.*

It all started when I received a call one weekend from a college buddy. I'll call him Jim. We had been keeping in touch for twenty years now, so I had every reason to think this was just another "kid update" or "fishing brag session." The tone in his voice, however, told me that this was not a routine call.

He said, "I am on the way to Colorado to see my parents." He hesitated. "I just found out," he reluctantly explained, "that I am being sued. The story is about to go public, and I wanted my parents to hear it from my own lips rather the gossip mill." He had been accused of a sexual impropriety that he had not done. I felt for his plight. Who will ever believe a pastor's claim of innocence in this day when stories of sexual misconduct are a daily occurrence?

He laid out the whole story. About an hour and a half later we said good-bye, and he promised to keep me posted.

A week or two later, he called to give me an update. I asked, "Jim, what did your folks say?"

"They said, 'Son, we have watched your life. We know who you are and what you are. Your life has been on display. We believe that you did not do it, because that would be out of character for who we know you to be. It simply does not square with what we know about you.'"

He also went to the West Coast to talk to the church body where he had formerly served and where the incident was being alleged. "What did they say?" I asked.

"They said, 'We know you and what kind of person you are. We don't believe it.'"

He went to his leadership and former staff members, who also responded in kind. They said, "We know your character. We will help you fight this, because we know you are innocent." One by one the circle of friends and associates stood up and testified to the portrait of his life.

There are a few occasions in life when the only thing you have to defend yourself is your character. As Proverbs 11:6 says, "Good character is the best insurance " (THE MESSAGE).

When the lawsuit came to trial, the accuser did not have any evidence and tried to paint the pattern of a man who is unfaithful. My friend's defense was easy. All he had to do was to simply pull out the canvas of the last twenty-five years and say, "Let's take a look." He could open up the private and public patterns of his life for public scrutiny, because he had nothing to hide. For twenty-five years of leadership and personal life, my buddy had never once been accused of anything of the kind. Not once had he been unfaithful. The grooves were consistent.

This was his character. He has been exonerated.

As the wisdom of Proverbs says, "A child is known by his doings, whether his work be pure, and whether it be right" (20:11 KJV). One of the boys in our neighborhood—I'll call him Travis—is known for lying to his parents. He will do whatever he can get away with. I have seen it again and again. When I confronted him one day with something inappropriate that my sons had told me he had done at our house, he was quick to deny it. "Travis," I said, "I do not trust you. I know that you lie. You can't fool me. You did it. I know it. Don't do it again." He was stunned. He was not used to someone calling his bluff. His defiance melted and he apologized. The sad thing will be if Travis grows up without ever learning that one's character—for good or bad—cannot be hidden. Johann Wolfgang von Goethe put it this way: "Behavior is a mirror in which everyone displays his own image."

So it is with character.

ERRANT BRUSH STROKES

Character is not about perfection. It does not mean a perfect record. None of us are perfect. It is not perfection, but the overall pattern, that is the point. There has never been a painter who did not have at least one misstroke on the canvas by the time it was done. There has never been a writer that did not go through bottles of Wite-out until someone invented the delete button.

Our friend King David was no exception. He needed Wite-out just like the rest of us. He had a wild, misguided stroke on his character canvas. There are two opposite reports that cause us to have serious conflict when it comes to the life of David. One is the comment that David was "a man after God's own heart." The other is the fact that David had adultery with Bathsheba and killed her husband to cover it up. How could David be characterized as a man with a heart for God when he was a murderous adulterer?

David was around fifty and had been king for almost twenty years when one day he fell to the lust of the eyes. The brush slipped in his hand and a blotch appeared on his canvas. Then he made the mess even bigger when he tried to cover it up and added murder to his rap sheet.

David did not set out to mess up. None of us ever do. One evening he was relaxing on his palace roof after a long day at work. Fatigue is almost always a factor in moral failure. As he channel surfed, looking out over Jerusalem, what should cross his field of vision but a naked woman taking a bath on a rooftop below? He liked what he saw. He wanted it.

He found out her name was Bathsheba. She was married to Uriah, one of David's soldiers who was off fighting at the front. Exercising his kingly authority, he summoned Bathsheba. When she came, he slept with her and she became pregnant with his child.

To cover it up, David had her husband, Uriah, recalled from

battle and gave him leave to come home and be with his wife, but Uriah refused to sleep with his wife while his fellow soldiers were fighting. David even got him intoxicated to overcome his resistance in hopes that Uriah would make love to his wife and thus cover David's tracks. Even under the fog of alcohol, Uriah rejected the comforts of home while his compatriots were risking their lives. As commentator Stuart Briscoe observed, "Uriah drunk was a better man than David sober."

David then panicked and orchestrated for Uriah to be assigned to the teeth of the battle in hopes he would be killed. Uriah willingly and unknowingly obeyed, going to the front line, where he was indeed killed. David was now free to marry Bathsheba. Months later the baby was born, and everything was back to normal. David thought he was in the clear. There was only one thing wrong: David had not dealt with his sin, and his heart had been ruptured. There is a great tendency and ability in all of us to camouflage our sin. Finally, God sent Nathan to confront David. Face-to-face with his guilt, David was grieved by what he had done, and repented.

I think we all would agree that David botched his canvas. He stumbled and failed in a big way. Nevertheless, when we see David in the book of Acts, it is not his failure that is remembered. In chapter 13 we are told, "I have found David son of Jesse a man after my own heart" (v. 22). In verse 36 it says David "served God's purpose in his generation." My point? When David's life was rehearsed for the generations to remember, it was not the rogue brushstroke of adultery chronicled in the book of Acts. Yes, he sinned, and yes, he stumbled. But one stumble is not a groove, and my character is bigger than a slip and fall. It is the pattern of my life. For David that overall pattern was a man who pursued the heart of God.

Am I excusing or ignoring the blotches on David's character?

Not at all. It took him almost a year to come to grips with the right steps of recovery. He had to carry some consequences of his sin the rest of his life. But there is a difference between slipping once and repeating the behavior over and over, creating a groove in your character.

As news columnist Marilyn vos Savant said, "An error becomes a mistake when we refuse to admit it." Proverbs 24:16 agrees: "Though a righteous man falls seven times, he rises again." David got back up. Character is not perfect, but when it falls, it gets back up.

REPENTING YOUR WAY TO BETTER CHARACTER

How do I build better, stronger character? Lesson one from David is, learn how to practice genuine repentance and accept genuine forgiveness. That double-barreled comment is easier said than done. In Psalm 51, we hear David's prayer of confession of his sin with Bathsheba and his plea for forgiveness: "Have mercy upon me, O God, according to thy lovingkindness: according unto the multitude of thy tender mercies blot out my transgressions. Wash me thoroughly from mine iniquity, and cleanse me from my sin" (vv. 1–2 KJV).

We must realize that we *are* going to mess up. It is what we do with that mess up that cuts the groove in our character. Abraham Lincoln once said, "My great concern is not whether you have failed, but whether you are content with your failure." It is not so much failure that forms character, but what we do after failure. Do we cover it up, ignore it, deny it, or do we admit it, walk toward it, and embrace personal change?

Oswald Sanders pointed out that "how men react *after* they have been sifted by Satan is a revelation of their true character.

For over a year and maybe longer, David remained in stubborn unwillingness to confess his sin. But ultimately the enormity of his sin was matched by the depth of his repentance."[1] David came to God and said, "I have messed up my portrait and need some Wite-out. Lord, I am not denying what I have done. But I want to move on if possible. Would You clean up the mistakes and allow me a fresh start?" God did, and the story ended with David back where he belonged with a repaired and clean heart.

David is a good example of setting and raising the character standard. Despite serious sins with Bathsheba and her husband, the way he dealt with his relationship to God and with other people and his own sin gives us a picture of a man after God's own heart.

OVERMANAGE YOUR ACHILLES

Many in the world of business today are like Achilles. Achilles was one of ancient Greek mythology's most famous warriors. He could conquer anything. Achilles owed thanks for his conquests to his mother. When he was born, she tried to make him immortal by dipping him in the river Styx, which made anything it touched invulnerable. This was the secret of Achilles' success.

Achilles also had a secret weakness. The heel that his mother held him by when dipping him in the river had remained dry and, as a result, unprotected. It was his weak spot. In the end he died as a result of an enemy's arrow that sliced the back of his foot. It opened a wound that would not heal and which eventually killed him. Achilles' heel was his downfall.

We all have an Achilles heel. It is crucial to our character that we know what it is and how to protect ourselves from its weakness. It has been my observation that we all struggle with one or two sins of the heart that are unique to our makeup. Although we are all theoretically vulnerable to all kinds of sin, there is almost always one sin of the heart that persistently stalks us.

That sin is different for everybody. As Oswald Sanders observed, "David's sensitive and artistic nature laid him open to temptation that would have bypassed one of a different texture."[2] This was David's Achilles heel. What is yours?

We have been guiding and coaching executives for over twenty-five years. We have noticed that many times there is one thing that an executives needs to grab by the horns and wrestle to the ground. Know your Achilles heel. Then manage it. Build boundaries to protect yourself from your own weakness.

OUR PATTERNS START EARLY AND STAY LONG

A liar starts lying early, a bully starts bullying early, and a manipulator starts manipulating early. Educators and counselors have known that for a long time. The rest of us are just now catching up.

An ancient Chinese proverb says, "Sow a thought, reap an act. Sow an act, reap a habit. Sow a habit, reap a character. Sow a character, reap a destiny." It is a truth that the Bible seconds: "Do not be deceived, God is not mocked; for whatever a man sows, this he will also reap" (Gal. 6:7 NASB).

Think about young teenage David suiting up to fight the giant. In the end we see a snapshot of his heart's motivation, what was *really* driving him. After the giant was lying on the ground, he did not strut around like some prizefighter who'd just taken the world title. He simply said, "Now all may know there is a God in Israel." That is character.

When did David become a giant slayer? It was long before, when he faced smaller challenges. When he got flock duty and his older brothers did not, he still obeyed his father, even though it did not seem fair. Sitting out in the field with the sheep all night, by himself, he chose to worship God to ward off his loneliness and fear. Fast-forward to when he was finally confronted with his adultery and murder. That day he slew a giant even bigger than Goliath. He faced and felled his own failure. This was perhaps his greatest bravery of all, admitting his own sin and setting it right.

Put those pieces together and you have a picture of a life. David as an adult was a man of humility, loyalty, courage, responsibility, and a soft, tender heart. A timeline of his life would root those character traits right back to his early years.

IT IS MY CHARACTER TO BUILD AND KEEP

Governing my character is very different from knowing my gift mix and internal wiring. Those were built into me by God when He created me. I am gifted and wired to be able to do certain things incredibly well. I am attracted to certain tasks and repelled by others. No matter how hard I work at improving my ability in certain areas, I may never be able to do them as well as someone else who is gifted and wired in different ways.

I do have control, however, over my character. I can improve it, modify it, or compromise it. In a world where we seem to have little control, we call the shots when it comes to whether or not our character is diminished. Job said to his friends concerning his character, "I will not deny my integrity. I will maintain my righteousness and never let go of it; my conscience will not reproach me as long as I live" (27:5–6).

If my character goes down, I am the only one who can be blamed. No other person apart from me can allow my character to be compromised. The first time I read this passage from Job, it hit me like a thunderbolt. I cannot blame anyone for my character erosion but myself. You cannot steal it from me. Only I can give up my character.

ONE STROKE AT A TIME

The first decade of the twenty-first century will undoubtedly be known in part for its rash of business scandals. CEOs talking up stock values while all the time selling their own shares on the side. Tawdry tales of money embezzled to pay for lavish birthday parties for their family members. Companies manipulating earning performance numbers by cooking the books. Unlike Reagan's era, this last ten years will probably be known in history as a time when corruption—not character—was king.

In the middle of the mess, *USA Today* did an article analyzing the signatures of accused executives. They brought in handwriting analysts to study the autographs of corporate defendants such as Sam Waksal, Jeff Skilling, and Ken Lay. According to the experts, Sam Waksal's deliberate strokes show intentionality. Dennis Kozlowski's big "D" shows the arrogance that led to his downfall. Andrew Fastow's illegible signature shows devious dissimilation.[3]

Although signature analysis is about as scientific as reading tarot cards, it is nonetheless true that each stroke of our lives goes to forming our character. We all are signing our names day after day as we live. Our character is carved one line at a time. The thing I must realize is that I am cutting grooves whether I think about it or not. A signature is being formed of some kind. What is the signature of my life and character? What is the signature of yours?

CHAPTER 15

No Overnight Delivery
on Character

YOU CANNOT DREAM YOURSELF INTO A CHARACTER; YOU MUST
HAMMER AND FORGE YOURSELF ONE.

—JAMES A. FROUDE

It was a Monday afternoon, and I was busy working my "to do" list. My secretary told me that my wife was on the line. In our office, family calls are always pushed through—regardless. Her call shook me to the very center of my life. Bill, one of my close friends, had suddenly been diagnosed with multiple myeloma, a form of bone cancer for which there is no known cure.

Bill is my age and has four boys—all still at home. He is a man after God's heart. We attend the same church, and our kids go to school together. Just last Friday night we had huddled side by side in warm blankets to watch a cold Arkansas high school football game.

Since that phone call that day, I have spent a lot of time with Bill. *I thought* it was so *I* could *help him* during this perilous journey. After a few short weeks, however, I realized that it was

I who was going to be the beneficiary of the relationship, not my friend.

I was amazed by how he responded to the threat of this enemy of his health. I was astonished at how this storm did not knock him down or even off course. He kept a constant heading. Yes, he had to reef in the sails for a fierce blow and batten down the hatches, but he and his family did not lose their footing. They plowed on.

He was dealing with this better than I was, and *he* was the one who was sick. How could he be handling this so well? It was a natural question. I knew my friend well, and the answer was clear. He was leaning on the character that he had been steadily building as long as I knew him. For me it was a lesson in character.

He had built his character day by day, decision by decision, over the years. Now it was there for him to lean on. Emergencies are not when you build character; they are when you spend the character you have already put in the bank. By the time you realize you need it, it's too late. Coming face-to-face with character on display in my cancer-ridden friend caused me to ask, "Where does this kind of character come from?"

I began to reflect deeper than I had in a long time on the issue of a man and his character. When and how had Bill, his wife, and even his children developed such strong, sturdy, personal and family character? From where does good character come? Walking with my friend through difficulty, it was now *my* character undergoing construction—not his.

THE HEART OF CHARACTER

For starters, good character is built on a good heart. Bill had a vibrant relationship with his God that had changed his heart. That was the core of his character. The most salient factor in Bill's circumstances was not the specific details of his cancer. No, it was the depth of his walk with God.

When Jesus was developing His team of leaders and preparing them for the adversity that He knew would come, He explained character development this way, "No good tree bears bad fruit, nor does a bad tree bear good fruit . . . The good man brings good things out of the good stored up in his heart, and the evil man brings evil things out of the evil stored up in his heart" (Luke 6:43, 45). Character is a fruit of the heart.

Where does a good heart come from? This is where conventional wisdom of leadership goes awry. It sees character as a muscle of leadership, when in truth, character is a muscle of the heart. Our culture is enamored with leadership, when it should be enamored with character.

Though every legitimate survey over the last few years consistently shows that integrity, honesty, and credibility are common characteristics of superior leaders, very few of them tie the condition of the heart to the stellar display of character.

Our culture, however, erroneously tries in vain to build a good heart apart from God. That is akin to trying to create a rainbow without resorting to beauty. The two are synonymous. One is the substance of the other. God is the fountainhead of all goodness. You cannot acquire character apart from connectedness to His character. He alone has the power to purify our hearts. Faith is crucial to character and leadership, because faith is the door to a renovated heart.

We cannot acquire these qualities simply by reading a book on "virtue" or listening to another speech on "being a successful leader." Good leaders have character that has grown from the soil of a good heart. What is in us comes out when we do "life at work."

Apart from God's spiritual intervention in our lives, the most that we can muster in the heart is a Potemkin village of morality.

Grigory Aleksandrovich Potemkin was an eighteenth-century Russian minister to the czarina Catherine the Great.

In 1789 Catherine decided to tour her empire down the Dneiper River through the Ukraine and Crimea. To impress Catherine with his administration of the region, Potemkin ordered that everything be hurriedly spruced up along the way. All of the countryside was furiously whitewashed. In their zeal to make a favorable impression on Catherine during her inspection tour down the river, Potemkin's bureaucrats created whole new villages that consisted only of fake pasteboard facades. They were a sham, a fraud.

Is your morality a "Potemkin village"?

Without the spiritual regeneration of God's Spirit, our best attempts at goodness and morality are no better. They may fool others around us for a time, but they are not the substance of real character. They are but feeble imitations. The framework for our heart to grow sound character comes only after God has touched it and turned it inside out.

THE CHARACTER-GROWING PROCESS

If character is what counts most, then it is critical that we build and protect a strong, pure heart. The heart is the seat of the inner person. It comprises feelings, desires, affections, motives, will, intellect, and principles. It is in the heart that we:

- initiate decision making
- process life
- ponder eternity
- filter negative emotions
- conquer sin cycles
- knit real friendships
- confirm personal significance

- engage in real worship
- transmit heritage to our children
- communicate to God

In short, as the book of Proverbs says, "As the heart goes, so we go" (paraphrase of Proverbs 23:7). The heart is where character is forged. After God gives each of us a new heart, it is up to us to water and nurture it. There are four factors to fostering a good heart that yield a bumper crop of good character:

RIGHT THINKING + TIME +
PRESSURE + GOOD DECISIONS = GOOD
CHARACTER

All four ingredients are necessary. There is no shortcut. Bypass any of them and character is short-circuited. My friend had character when it counted, because he had paid his dues on all fronts. Let's examine each of these components.

RIGHT THINKING

Technological and economic change has transformed the world of our work. The boom of the nineties rode that wave. It seemed everyone was riding high. Salaries rose steadily. All were in the "buy" mode. Companies were. Consumers were. Mutual funds too. Our 401(k)s kept growing in value. The possibilities of the "new economy" seemed limitless. Customers seemed to be falling off the trees. Speculators abounded. Technology had changed everything. Business raced to keep up with the unfolding frontiers of the information age.

Then there was the bust. The bubble broke. It was not just tech stocks that collapsed. Nor was the crisis merely a matter of unemployment figures, stalled GNP, or rising deficits. Although global outsourcing, layoffs, and joblessness followed, they were not the worst of it all. Though all of these dominated the news, there was an even bigger bust that hit offices across the country. The most fundamental failure was the moral bankruptcy of the American workplace. This age of business had lost its moral bearing. There is no character without a moral compass of right thinking.

During the same period of wild prosperity in the nineties, a technological revolution was reshaping the world of navigation as well. It was the development of a satellite-based navigation system called the GPS that could pinpoint your location anywhere on the globe to within several feet.

The GPS fundamentally changed the way ships keep from getting lost for the first time since the inventions of the magnetic compass and the sextant. With a GPS a captain could instantly know exactly where he was, the precise direction that his ship was heading, and the speed of his real forward progress.

A little while after the GPS came into wide usage, an odd thing happened. Maritime insurance companies began to notice an increase in loss claims due to ships running aground. An unusually high number of ships were wrecking. How could this be? Navigation had never been easier, or more precise. Never before had so much piloting information been so accessible. Why would a technological revolution that removed so many barriers to safety lead to such catastrophic failures?

The reason, it turned out, was elementary. The problem had to do with maps. Many captains, it seems, stopped looking at the map. They punched in their destination coordinates into the GPS and put the ship on autopilot. Not unlike the business world, they thought that technology would give them an easy ride. The GPS did what it was good at. It took their ships on a straight line from point A to point B, just as it had been told. The only problem was that the GPS could not read maps. No one was thinking.

When one captain punched the coordinates of his next port into his GPS and went below to work on something else, his vessel hit its target—literally. The GPS drove it directly into the correct harbor and right up on land. Another ship's commander used the coordinates of a navigation buoy where he needed to go. The GPS did its job and ran straight into the buoy. Many ships ran aground because no one noticed that the straight line of electronic navigation crossed hazards clearly marked on paper maps: rocks, shallows at low tide, even rock jetties. Without reference to a map, electronic navigation too frequently found itself high and dry.

The American way of work and business has similarly run aground. The ethical foundering of so many companies and individuals is not surprising when the SOP is to navigate freely, following the winds of promotion, profit, and stock price without regard to the moral mapping of right and wrong. We knew where it was, where it wanted to go, and how to get there. We thought that was enough. We hit hazards we did not know were there because we were going full speed ahead without a map.

Working without faith is like using a GPS without a map. You may very well be in motion. You may even feel you are getting somewhere. Just prepare for a jarring wake-up when the course you are on hits the hard-wired moral reality of the cosmos. If you operate loosely with legal details, don't be surprised when your partner cheats you. If you lie to clients, don't be surprised when your suppliers lie to you. Don't complain to the ref when the way you were playing communicated that anything was fair game.

Many people redefine right and wrong on the job to suit their present needs. Then they wonder why they run aground when it comes back to bite them. They are working very hard on a faulty definition of honesty or integrity or diligence or loyalty. The problem is their lack of right thinking.

Faith provides the critical moral map to our work. It tells us how to think rightly about what we are doing. We will talk more fully in the next few chapters on how to do this by building a moral warehouse of right thinking.

TIME

Growing character also requires time. The day my friend was diagnosed with cancer did not destroy his world, because his character had the momentum built over time. It was not easily stopped. Time is either your friend or your enemy, depending on how you have spent it. Time is the enemy of a life wasted, but it is the friend of a life like my friend's that has been consistently invested.

Character comes in bits and pieces, not as a complete package. David's character was forged over many years and at least four careers. Early in his career he was very quick to take offense and revenge. When Nabal refused to feed David and his men in 1 Samuel 25, David's hair-trigger response to the four hundred soldiers under his command was: "Put on your swords!" (v. 13). Nabal would have died an ugly death had his wife, Abigail, not personally intervened and begged David to leave her husband alone. Now contrast that event with one much later in David's kingship, when a man named Shimei cursed David as he fled from his palace and the city of Jerusalem. How did David respond with the benefit of some gray hair?

> David then said to Abishai and all his officials, "My son, who is of my own flesh, is trying to take my life. How much more, then, this Benjamite! Leave him alone; let him curse, for the LORD has told him to. It may be that the LORD will see my distress and repay me with good for the cursing I am receiving today." So David and his men continued along the road while Shimei was going along the hillside opposite him,

cursing as he went and throwing stones at him and showering him with dirt. (2 Sam. 16:11–13)

David had grown over the years. Building character is a day-by-day, lifetime commitment. As we allow the Holy Spirit to work in our lives and chip away at our character one piece at a time, we will change over time. Our character will improve. David's character did not look the same before as it did after.

In the area where I live, land is constantly being cleared for new subdivisions. The trees are cut down, leaving bald earth. Then the houses are built. Finally, new landscaping is put in. Store-bought trees, however, are pathetic when compared to the mature specimens that had once grown there. It takes years for a full-gloried maple or oak to sprawl across someone's front yard. And it takes years for mature character to be built. As Samuel Johnson said, "Excellence, in any department, can only be attained by the labor of a lifetime. It is not purchased at a lesser price."

Time builds character, and time tests character as well.

My partner and I have been in business together for well over a decade. At the very beginning of our association, we laid out common core values to help define our relationship with each other as well as to define the behavior of our organization. Those values include statements such as "We will improve each other" and "We will finish well."

We are very different men today than we were twelve years ago. Our characters have been tested. They have improved. In the context of our work world, we have confronted—and continue to confront—issues such as controlling anger, keeping promises, treating colleagues as valued assets, and telling the truth. We deal with our egos and defensiveness, our ambition and stress. Our work world is a laboratory for the improvement of our character. Every work situation is. It is often not easy; but it is always valuable. As the famous opera soprano Beverly Sills once observed: "There are no shortcuts to anyplace worth going."

Every single day of our work lives, we take hundreds of actions. We make behavior choices scores of times. When we sum up all of those individual behaviors over an hour, then a day, then a week, then a month, then a decade, we have patterns of behavior. Those patterns of behavior make up our character.

We Americans like everything done fast. Charles Swindoll observed, "We love to promote an independent spirit without ever considering the value of time-forged character. God never promotes like that. God takes time. When God plans to use us, He puts us through the paces."[1] Our society has yet to learn that you cannot microwave character. There is no substitute for time.

PRESSURE

One of the forces shaping character over time is the pressure of suffering. It usually takes years for the natural course of a river to turn. Year after year, erosion cuts its banks, creating a new and different path. If, however, you take the same river and apply sustained pressure, its course could change in a day. Seven days of flooding will alter the flow of the river. Fly over the Mississippi and you will see telltale remnants of such catastrophic change. It meanders like a snake, but all along its course are the oxbow lakes and channels of its former riverbed. When the rains come and the water rises, there is always a new landscape after it recedes back into its banks. Difficulty changes you for good or bad.

My friend Bill had successfully faced many difficulties over his life. Each of these prepared him for the battle of his life. Just as carbon does not become a diamond without pressure, character is likewise never fully formed apart from weathering life's tests.

When I was a boy, we had this plastic thing that you inserted into the core of an orange. It had a straw that you could then use to suck the juice out. I would squeeze those oranges every which way to get every last succulent drop. I would suck oranges until my lips burned from the citric acid. A mentor of mine used to say that when you get squeezed, whatever is in you will come out. Bill was being squeezed, and squeezed hard, but what came out was pure, 100 percent character. Be assured, the content of our hearts will be tested. Character is always tested.

Work has a way of squeezing all of us. From those pressure points come our reflexes and reactions. It is our responses to circumstances that publicize what is in our hearts. Today's workplace is even less stable and more uncertain than it used to be. In the last couple of years I have observed a number of people who received the dreadful news that they were losing their jobs. Always, however, their character has shown through.

It was the week before Christmas—believe it or not—when Robert, another of my friends, found out that the following Friday would be his last day with his company. This man had been with his company a long time. He had poured his talents into it and was rewarded well. Suddenly, those at the top felt it would be financially and strategically shrewd to dissolve two departments. "Robert, your job is gone. Merry Christmas."

He called me and we met for a quick lunch as he replayed the story. I remember saying to him, "So, Robert, what are you going to do?" He looked back with a little hesitation and said, "I'm going to take about a week and do some 'heart work.'"

I asked, "What do you mean by that?"

He said, "I want to make sure I learn what I need to learn in this situation. I want to make sure that this situation makes me a better man, not a bitter man. I don't want to rationalize away some of the feedback points, nor do I want to build a wall of resentment and revenge toward my company and my boss.

"Most of all, I want to make sure that I guard myself from a quick reflex of 'I've got to go out and fix my problem.' I want to make sure that I am genuinely trusting the Lord as I dust off my résumé—which I haven't done in almost twenty years—and start knocking on doors." Robert was using adversity to squeeze every drop of personal growth from his circumstances that he could. That is a reflex of character. It comes from a heart committed to what is good.

Someone—I do not remember who—once said, "How a man plays the game shows something of his character; how he loses shows all of it." All of us react when suffering hits—for good or bad. Some people react with denial. "This can't be happening to me," they say, burying their heads in the sand. Some people react with a kind of redirection or escapism. "I'll just go fishing all weekend, or hit happy hour two hours early, or lose myself in a good book."

Others are pessimists from birth. Everyone knows a couple of these people. Every time you see them, they're singing a different verse of "Nobody Knows the Trouble I've Seen." And then others respond with a shallow kind of optimism. "Well, I guess I'll just have to grin and bear it."

My friends Bill and Robert soberly embraced their trials. The epistle of James says it this way: "Consider it pure joy, my brothers, whenever you face trials of many kinds, because you know that the testing of your faith develops perseverance. Perseverance must finish its work so that you may be mature and complete, not lacking anything" (1:2–4). Tough times come to all of us. Different shapes, different sizes, different weights, but they will come. The Bible acknowledges that as a fact of life. How we receive and digest suffering can become one of the greatest shapers of our character.

Some things come through the pressure of suffering that cannot and will not come any other way. The apostle Paul explained how he coped with the tragedies of his life: "We also rejoice in our sufferings, because we know that suffering produces perseverance; perseverance, character; and character, hope" (Rom. 5:3–4). Robert Browning put it this way:

> I walked a mile with Pleasure,
>   She chattered all the way,
> But she left me none the wiser,
>   For all she had to say.
> I walked a mile with Sorrow,
>   And ne'er a word said she;
> But, oh, the things I learned from her
>   When Sorrow walked with me![2]

We do not like the stress of crisis. No one asks for more pressure on their lives. Yet when it comes, it is a strategic opportunity to strengthen your character.

Good Decisions

I can have right thinking and time and pressure doing their magic, but it is the decisions I make in the moment that ultimately matter. My character development many times comes down to a single choice. It is the instant when I have to choose the good over the bad, the right over the wrong, and the true over the false. I have to act. Something must be done, but what?

The ability to make right decisions is called "wisdom." Wisdom is knowledge rightly applied. Character results from a series of wise decisions. Choosing wisely requires not only knowledge of right and wrong and an accurate appraisal of the situation, but also the discernment of what principles to bring to bear and what they conclude. It also requires the fortitude to do what ought to be done, no matter how difficult it is.

Today's business climate thrives on something called wisdom—that really isn't. It feeds on the wisdom of the street, prevailing wisdom, also known as conventional wisdom. The wisdom of the crowd is not true wisdom at all, but merely consensus. It is a polled opinion. All it tells you is which way the wind is blowing. Most of what pass for decisions today aren't decisions, but weather readings. Real wisdom in decision making looks beyond what everyone seems to think. It looks for what is right, what is best, what is good, no matter what the consequences or opposition.

A good decision must have wisdom to go on, but it also needs timely execution. In baseball the umpire only has a few seconds from the time the ball crosses the plate until he must make the call. Any delay in his judgment could be fatal. There is only one thing fans hate worse than a bad call. It is a bobbled call. One that is not made decisively.

Make the call.

General George Patton kept a list of the principles he used to lead. They were collected in a booklet titled *Patton's Principles*. One of them states that there comes a point in every decision in which further deliberation becomes counterproductive and a decision needs to be made. Additional information always has a curve of diminishing return. There is always a tipping point at which the benefit of more analysis is outweighed by the opportunity cost of delay.[3]

To not make a decision is to make a decision. Yes, committing yourself to one option closes the door on others. Hesitation, however, is a habit of poor character. Decision making is a muscle. It atrophies when not used. It must become an instinct. A will to act and act wisely is at the core of what character means. Leo J. Muir concurred when he wrote, "Character is a subtle thing. Its sources are obscure, its roots delicate and invisible. We know it when we see it and it always commands our admiration, and the absence of it our pity; but it is largely a matter of will." There is no character where there is no will to act.

CAN YOU FEDEX IT TO ME?

When the front doorbell rings, followed by the sound of a delivery truck driving off, we know that a mysterious package has arrived and is leaning against the door, awaiting our retrieval. Overnight delivery is amazing, isn't it? I can order a computer program tonight from halfway across the country, and it will be sitting on my front porch tomorrow morning. Character is not like that. It does not just show up all neatly wrapped on the front porch. Character is not available in a catalogue. You cannot order it online. It is not a mail-order proposition. Character, however, is delivered. It comes from a heart changed by God that has been fertilized with four essential nutrients: Right thinking. Time. Pressure. Good decisions.

CHAPTER 16

CONSTRUCTING A MORAL WAREHOUSE

EFFECTIVENESS WITHOUT VALUES IS A TOOL WITHOUT A PURPOSE.

—EDWARD DE BONO

Sam Walton defied the odds. While other mass retailers like K-Mart, Montgomery Ward, and Rose's were all hemorrhaging financially, Walton built the Wal-Mart empire, the world's largest chain of general merchandise stores. His competitors' dingy and tattered stores felt crowded, dirty, and hostile—like the feeling you get when you walk into the license bureau. You had to wait in line to buy overpriced stuff from grumpy people. Walton knew he could do better.

Walton's stores were big, open, and clean, with a smiling face greeting you at the door. His discount prices were not blue-light specials, an exception to the rule. Instead, everything in the store was sold as cheaply as he could possibly get it.

You cannot fully appreciate what Sam Walton did, however, until you have been to a Third World country and experienced its poverty, then return home and walk the aisles of a Wal-Mart. Aisle after aisle of shelves lined with every species of stuff you could ever imagine. The plethora of products waiting to be bought and consumed is overwhelming. What is more, it is all waiting in a store within easy driving distance of you, no matter what corner of this country you live in. Walton pulled off what no other retailer in the world ever did quite so well: offering you everything you need, in stock and at your fingertips, and all at "Every-Day Low Prices."

It would be hard to say which was faster: other stores closing or Walton's stores going up. They were dying on the vine while the Wal-Mart Super Center was popping up everywhere. Wal-Mart took over like kudzu. From one store in Rogers, Arkansas, in 1962, it has now grown to over forty-three hundred Wal-Mart associated facilities around the globe. In 2003, Wal-Mart became the number one Fortune 500 Company. In 2004, it was rated one of the most admired companies in America.

It must be doing something right. There is a secret to Wal-Mart's success that you will never see in its stores. It is—surprisingly—the Wal-Mart warehouse. Walton knew that one of the keys to unlocking success in retail is found in how you keep and distribute stock. There can be no store without a successful system of distribution.

Two contradictory facts have long haunted retail. On the one hand, you cannot sell a product that you do not stock. Keeping stuff on the shelves is crucial. On the other hand, inventory costs you money every day that it just sits. Wal-Mart solved this dilemma by developing a state-of-the-art warehousing and distribution system using technology resulting in just-in-time delivery.

You will never see an empty shelf at Wal-Mart. Nevertheless, if you stayed and watched one of its shelves, either in the store or in its warehouses, you would never see merchandise sitting for long.

The Wal-Mart distribution centers around the country are one of the keys to their low prices. Wal-Mart has learned how to buy, merchandise, and move stuff more efficiently than anyone in the world.

A Wal-Mart warehouse and distribution center is something to behold. Fifty acres of land are needed for its eight hundred thousand square feet of warehousing space—one of the largest one-roof footprints there is. The truckloads of goods never cease coming in and out at its forty-five-plus shipping docks. Six hundred employees work day and night receiving freight, tracking it, and dispatching it as needed to go directly to store shelves. On any given day they handle $10 million worth of inventory. In a year Wal-Mart's warehouses ship over $244 billion worth of merchandise worldwide.

Wal-Mart invests $55 million dollars to construct each of its distribution centers for one reason: you have to stock before you can sell. You cannot retail what you have not invested in wholesale.

This simple principle is just as true for our work lives. Character has to have a moral warehouse from which to draw. Constructing a moral warehouse is a critical infrastructure for God-intended Life@Work. Are you regularly investing in your moral warehouse? If we have not put systems in place that keep our souls well stocked, we should not be surprised when we show up at the store one day and find the shelves empty.

A moral warehouse is not just static virtue. It is not enough to be a good person today. Just thinking that you know right from wrong will only get you so far. Instead, just as in warehousing and distribution, character depends on an ongoing process. It must constantly be replenished. Its inventory needs ongoing management.

Too often those who discuss moral character only talk about the virtues themselves—honesty, loyalty, perseverance, courage, etc. What can be neglected is the process by which such personal strengths are acquired and built into one's life. Walton knew that if he built the infrastructure, the goods would flow. Similarly, building a moral warehouse is more about life habits that stock character than it is about the specific character qualities themselves. Life is just like in *The Field of Dreams*: "If you build it, they will come."

Four activities are helpful in the construction, the utilization, and the replenishment of the moral warehouse: constructing personal convictions, capturing inspirational moments, conducting Scripture memory, and connecting with people of character.

CONSTRUCTING PERSONAL CONVICTIONS

It has been said that an opinion is something you hold, whereas a conviction is something that holds you. One of the most evidential ways for character to be expressed in a person's life begins with having sound, solid, personal principles to live by. We call those convictions. What is a conviction? *A conviction is a category of God's thinking on a particular area or issue that I wholeheartedly embrace and act upon with determination.*

Our warehouse needs to be stocked with timeless axioms and values that do not change. There is only one place to get an unbiased perspective not subject to human whim. The only such source is God Himself. Building a conviction begins with discovering exactly what God thinks and has had to say about a topic or issue that I might be wrestling with. And to that we have good news. I don't need to sit around and wonder about God's thinking, because it has been recorded in the book called the Bible. Abraham Lincoln spoke with wisdom when he said, "The best gift God has given man is the Bible."

When it comes to the Bible being the foundation for modern practical life, two guidelines hold the sides of the conversation. First, we ought to remember that there is not a specific verse for every occurrence in life to give me a black-and-white guidebook on my journey. But second, almost every core area of life is touched on by a principle, proverb, or illustration found somewhere in the Bible.

There is no such thing as an inactive conviction. Character is never passive. Every personal conviction needs to show up to fight. Every personal principle eventually will be called out and tested. Moral challenges are always battles won or lost by the will.

Perhaps no biblical example has more to say about the concept of living from convictions than Daniel. Somewhere, somehow, when he was young, he had developed a belief system. We know nothing of his parents, but they must have done a good job. Daniel, like all of us, however, had to stand on his own two feet. Already by his teenage years, his convictions were being tested at a level that would have disqualified many adult Christians.

1. SOMETIMES THE BIGGEST TEST OF OUR CONVICTIONS COMES WHEN WE ARE DETACHED FROM OUR COMFORTABLE CHRISTIAN SUBCULTURE. Daniel was a Jew taken captive—kidnapped to a foreign country—and forced to work for a hostile foreign kingdom. Daniel had been uprooted from his native land and transplanted into an alien environment. All of his external anchors had been stripped. Yet Daniel remained grounded in his own convictions and character. The first chapter of Daniel records his resolve: "But Daniel made up his mind that he would not defile himself with the king's choice food or with the wine which he drank" (v. 8). Daniel would not compromise his faith by eating unkosher food, not even to curry favor with his captors.

Christians today face a similar challenge. Life on Sunday in the confines of the church building is an easier assignment than life on Monday at the office. We work in an office culture as foreigners. What we do there and the choices we make—not what we say—will define us. Like Daniel, our faith is tested daily by the moral dilemmas of pagan culture. For those who travel with their jobs, they know the particular temptations and challenges that you face in a culture that has no moral boundaries. If you do not know who you are, you will be forever confused about the choices you face. Daniel knew he was a Jew. For him that meant many decisions did not have to be made; they were already decided by his identity.

2. THE CULTURE WILL CHALLENGE OUR CHRISTIAN CONVICTIONS. Young Daniel was offered food that as a Jew he was not supposed to eat. He was given a new education, and his overlords even changed his name. His environment had done everything possible to soften his firm stand on right and wrong. But he did not break. As a matter of fact, he did not even bend.

A belief must be tested to be enshrined as a conviction. All of the inventory of our moral warehouse will eventually go through quality control. If it is not genuine, it will not pass. If there is anything an unbelieving work culture will smell out, it is lack of authenticity. Your colors will be shown whether you like it or not. You cannot hide your character. Your convictions—good, bad, or indifferent—will come into play. All of the choices you face every day make sure of that.

3. THE DISPLAY OF FIRM CHRISTIAN CONVICTIONS DOES NOT HAVE TO BE OBNOXIOUS AND DISGUSTING. Daniel did not say, "I'm a Jew, you idiot; I can't eat your food." Instead, he balanced his convictions with his desire to have positive influence and impact. This is a difficult truth for many Christians to accept. Conviction requires not just boldness, but it also has to have meekness and discretion. Conviction makes a stand not because it wants to, but because it has to. It tries to do so quietly. It does not call attention

to itself. It speaks more with its actions than it does its words. If Daniel did not have this kind of winsome witness, he could not have survived to serve four different administrations.

In our book *The Power of One*,[1] we addressed the very topic of being a "power of one" in a chapter titled "Standing Up Without Always Standing Out." Christians make a fatal mistake when they think that their alien morality means they must live and work as oddballs. We may be outsiders morally, but it is a tactical error to let the template of being an outsider define us socially at the office. Integrating your faith and work does not mean hitting coworkers over the head with a ten-pound gilded King James Bible. Nothing could be more damaging spiritually than a socially challenged Christian at the office, armed with truth but clueless about humility and love. This reminds me of what Adlai Ewing Stevenson once said, "It is often easier to fight for principles than to live up to them."

4. Holding to clear biblical convictions always carries consequences. A display of character starts with a man or woman knowing what is right and wrong. You build the steel frame for sturdy character and sound, consistent decision making on the base of deep-seated, personalized truth. It ends with some kind of consequence. The result might be quiet or unseen to the mass public. Or it might be visible for all to see the outcome of my convictions.

I have learned that some people get worse the more we get to know them; others just unfold depth upon depth. The more we peel back, the more we find that impresses us. One of my partners met a gentleman at a strategic planning summit our company was leading for one of our clients. My partner commented, "This is a great guy. We need to spend more time with him." This man was clearly on the deep end of the pool in his character.

A few months later we had the occasion of spending the morning with him on the East Coast. Through the conversation that morning, we learned that the man had been very financially successful years ago. But when the market turned, he had lost everything and ended up owing creditors more than sixty million dollars. Though he knew he would have to struggle to make it, he also knew that he had to pay back every dollar. So he constructed a payback plan, contacted everyone, and pledged his word to clear his debt.

Last year he made his last payment for a twenty-thousand-dollar debt to a small bank in the Southeast. He personally drove to the bank and handed the check to the banker, who said, "I thought you would never do this." This modern-day Daniel said, "I didn't have a choice. It was the right thing to do. I knew it years ago, and it has never left me." His convictions had consequences. The circumstance of bankruptcy called them out. He would either pay back what he owed or he wouldn't. Either way he had to show his colors.

Have you developed any convictions that shape and guide your work life? What are they? Take out a piece of paper and write out the ten most active convictions that apply to your work life. Make sure they are rooted in Scripture. Without them, we will be what James describes as "a doubting man unsettled as a wave of the sea that is driven and tossed back and forth by the wind" (James 1:6).

CAPTURING INSPIRATIONAL MOMENTS OF LIFE

There are times and moments in life that are pregnant with meaning. These are those times that hit us in the gut: the birth of a child, graduations, weddings, funerals, promotions, layoffs, achievements, or perhaps failures. I am talking about life milestones. It is usually when something externally has caused us to pull over internally for some reflection. We pause and drink in life a little slower than usual. We call these *transformational encounters.*

Life's significant moments are opportunities that should not be missed. They provide the chance to inventory our moral warehouses. It could be sitting out on the porch, watching the sun go down. It could be a close call or an accident. It could be a scare or a thrill. It could be attached to a day away or a vacation. A song can do it. A sight can trigger it. A memory can hit the switch. An annual review could do it.

Our country had such a wake-up call on September 11, 2001. The national tragedy of the World Trade Center terrorist attacks stopped us all in our tracks. We all took what I call a 9-11 review. That day, something suddenly invaded our routines and snapped us awake from the slumber of our work-a-day life. The ephemeral was vaporized. The extraneous quickly fell to the ground. All that was left is what really matters. It was one of those times when what really counts is brought poignantly to the fore. The real substance of life is so clear that you can almost touch it. September 11 was a transformational moment.

Transformational moments are not always tragedies. They can just as easily be personal triumphs. The point is not the drama, but the teachable moment that life provides us.

We pause and inhale and contemplate. It is a time when we reorder our private worlds, a time when we realign our belief systems with our behavior. It is at these moments in life that we do some of our best character review and alignment.

CONDUCTING SCRIPTURE MEMORY

The discipline and practice of Scripture memory has been lost with my generation. I do not think it is an overstatement to suggest that we now have a whole cohort growing up without a firsthand knowledge of the Scripture. I love modern worship, and I love progressive churches. I prefer practical sermons and fun, creative narratives, but here is one man's observation: we no longer engage the Scriptures directly.

Scripture memory is not difficult. Like working out, it just requires an investment of a few minutes each day. There are many resources designed to get you started. But you can easily begin on your own. Stop and make a list of the current concerns on your plate of life, whatever they may be: perhaps a difficult boss, your son's bad grades, conflict with your husband over finances, a test report of the presence of cancer, the uncertainty of a job transition. Now take these concerns to Scripture.

I continue to be amazed to discover that the Bible has so much to say regarding so many topics. We have a standing joke in our family about the fact that the Bible even tells us how to take care of pets. Proverbs 27:23 says, "Know the condition of your flocks and put your heart into caring for your herd." You will be surprised to find that the Bible has much to say specifically to what you are facing as well.

Unfortunately, many people still see the Bible as a book for preachers to use for a Sunday sermon or a collection of Christian superheroes only for children. It might be that, but the original intention of God in the collection of this magnificent book was to provide wisdom, guidance, and encouragement for each of us every day in the details of life.

CONNECTING WITH PEOPLE OF CHARACTER

Good character keeps good company.

We all know this to be true when we are young; we just forget that it's still true as we get older. I can remember my mom instructing me to stay away from Jimmy down the street. "He's a rotten apple," she would say. (Of course, we wonder how many moms were saying that about us back then.) We all know what that means. It means the same thing that Paul meant when he said decisively, "Bad company corrupts good character" (1 Cor. 15:33). But who cautions us of rotten apples when life graduates us to our twenties, thirties, forties, and beyond?

I sat down the other day and analyzed all the relationships in my personal world. In honor of my mother, I sorted them out into four apple categories. There were healthy apples, bruised apples, rotten apples, and poisonous apples.

Walter was self-employed. Even as a youngster, people noticed his entrepreneurial bent. His latest career was the launching of his own communication and advertisement company. He had landed a big first account that hurled him forward. Starting strong was never Walter's problem.

It was sometime after year four that his wife first asked Walter why he was slowly changing and becoming someone different from the man she had married. His reflex response was that she was making it all up and that they both were just getting older. Then the kids started making comments too. Finally, a couple of his best friends began probing.

As the story unraveled, the rotten apple was exposed. Walter had experienced a surge of growth in his third year of business and—as always—business growth takes capitalization. Walter could not self-fund the opportunities that lay ahead of them. And like any red-blooded American entrepreneur, he put together a "deal" to bring in some outside investors.

Evidently his only criterion for an investor was "anyone who would give him lots of money." As it turned out, he partnered with a man who had none of Walter's values and none of Walter's convictions. Eventually someone was going to affect someone, and in the long run Walter was the one affected. As a friend of mine used to say, "If you go to bed with a dog, don't be surprised when you wake up with the fleas."

Walter began to use language that his family had never heard from his mouth. He began a slow unraveling of many of his best qualities—patience, kindness, and even honesty. It came to a confrontation when his wife and one of his key employees called Walter's hand on his handling of the company's income tax. He was cheating and lying to cover it up.

Healthy relationships reinforce strong character; unhealthy relationships destroy it.

KEEPING THE VITAL LIFELINE FLOWING

Southern California is a veritable paradise. Its balmy weather and rolling hills overlooking the Pacific Ocean have attracted ever-increasing numbers of transplants from across America. Swanky neighborhoods with their irrigated green grass and lush landscaping make it an enticing place to move.

If you drive into the greater Los Angeles area from Arizona, the sudden visual transition from brown to dark green leaves no doubt that you are entering a desert oasis. The eastward spread of its new hilltop stucco villas with their terra-cotta roofs still continues as sand and scrub become street, sidewalk, and lawn.

Los Angeles's growth, however, has had one principal problem from the very beginning: water. It sits in an arid watershed. Its annual rainfall is insufficient for its needs. Seasonal drought means that what rain it does get is inconsistent. There is no reservoir within its city limits to quench its growing suburban thirst.

One hundred years ago its citizens and civic leaders realized they needed a reliable outside supply of water. Plenty of water existed in the watershed of western America. It just did not flow to Southern

California. To get it there would require an artificial infrastructure. Southern Californians began buying water rights and building canals and pipelines to get the water they needed from the mountains to their growing urban metropolis. Eventually they built three major aqueducts. The Colorado River Aqueduct runs over 300 miles, bringing water from high in snow pack off the mountains of Wyoming and Colorado to the California coast. The two Los Angeles aqueducts draw water over 360 miles from the snowmelts of the Sierras in Northern California.

These aqueducts are the lifelines of Southern California. They deliver over four and a half billion gallons of water per year. Government officials predict, however, that if its population continues to grow at the present rate, it will outstrip its supply, and by 2010 it will have a shortage of one to two billion gallons of water per year.

It is a simple fact that you cannot grow what you do not water. Furthermore, you cannot water where you have no irrigation system. The same is true with character. Integrity requires an infrastructure. It must be constantly nurtured and resupplied. Doing so requires intentional lifelong investment. It means building character-sustaining habits. There is no shortcut. There is no point of arrival. Personal growth always requires an ever-deeper reservoir.

Southern California cannot grow without an infrastructure supplying it water. Wal-Mart cannot sell without a distribution system. You will never have any character to display if you do not first have a moral warehouse. Start building yours now.

CONCLUSION

The Church@Work

I BELIEVE ONE OF THE NEXT GREAT MOVES OF GOD IS GOING TO
BE THROUGH THE BELIEVERS IN THE WORKPLACE.

—Dr. Billy Graham

Just yesterday a report came my way on our old friend Charles Antonio Bordini III. It has been eighteen months since my encounter with him in that Chicago boardroom when he confronted getting "the two Charlies" into the same earth suit. I am happy to report that he is still going full throttle. He is still very much commercial, still very much kingdom—still very much Charlie. Only now he lives and works out of a life that is whole. Charlie is but one of a growing legion of Christians we meet across the country who are rediscovering the doubly sharp Life@Work for which God made them.

CHARLIE FOUND A POWERFUL LIFE@WORK

As it was for Charlie, it is critical that we correctly see and sort out the four landscapes of our church life, our family life, our civic life, and our work life. Why? If I think that my commercial world is only there to support, resource, and platform the professional ministry of the church, I will undercut my calling and have no incentive to keep my skill set sharp. If I see my job always as the enemy of my church or my family, I will always be operating in a vocation shortfall. If all I see of my work is a paycheck, I will not view it as part of my wider involvement with my community. If I do not squarely stake down what work can and should do for me, it will run recklessly across the other parts of my Life@Work. It is impossible to sustain a balanced and successful Life@Work without putting the church, family, and work in their proper arrangement.

As Charlie learned, work itself must be reforged, integrating my kingdom commitment with my commercial calling. To do that I must understand, appreciate, and approach work correctly. It was the world of work where Charlie was facing his painful disconnect. It was there that Charlie had to navigate the myths and misconceptions that often derail even the most purposeful followers of Jesus.

After LASIK-like corrective surgery of these blind spots in his vision, Charlie was finally ready to begin the process of rebuilding his Life@Work. Through understanding and employing the four tools of *delivering skill, evidencing calling, modeling serving,* and *displaying character,* Charlie was able to flesh out the ideas of integration and impact. For him those four tools pried open the box of optimum internal fulfillment, external maximum impact, and passionate pleasure in God.

"VERY, VERY"

The Washington, D.C., meeting brought together about thirty followers of Christ, who also happened to be high-level business leaders. Here was a whole roomful of Charlies from across the country. They had flown in to pursue a greater understanding of servant leadership.

As the meeting wore on, an interesting pattern developed. Whenever the talk focused on business, these leaders dove in with full force and great self-assurance. They talked about P and Ls, marketing strategies, management theories, market trends, branding, and strategic analysis. They reeled off data and statistics the way a baseball fanatic quotes the batting averages of his favorite players.

When the talk turned to theology or Scripture, however, these well-educated, business-savvy leaders invariably prefaced everything they said with an apology: "I'm not a theologian," they would say, "but I think . . ." Or, "I'm not a professional pastor, but it seems like . . ." When it was time to talk about business, they were very eager to explain what they *knew*. But when the time came to talk about God, they hesitated to even venture what they *thought*.

Why would otherwise confident business leaders hedge their statements about the most important area of their lives? For most of them, it was not biblical competency but confidence that they lacked. These marketplace leaders did not feel equipped to make a spiritual assertion about their work. They are called as priests to their daily world, yet they stammered when it came time to say, "Thus saith the Lord . . ." about business.

Have you ever been to a chiropractor or physical therapist who did an arm-resistance test? They have you hold both arms straight out from your side. They then push down on each arm one at a time while you push back up in resistance. If one side is weaker than the other in its push back, it is a sign of spinal misalignment. These business leaders had a weak push-back on the faith side of their lives. This, too, is an alignment problem. If they saw their work and their faith aligned, both sides would be equally confident.

Scripture calls us to be "very, very" men and women. Our privilege and responsibility is to be very Bible and very business.

Many folks we meet are either "very business, sort of Bible" or "sort of business, very Bible." A "very, very" person is one who consistently develops a growing expertise in both Bible and business. Being successful in my Life@Work is all about exploring and understanding a "very, very" world and becoming a "very, very" disciple with both confidence and credibility.

New believers are the only people with a legitimate reason to say, "I don't know the Bible very well." Anyone who has been in the faith for a few years ought to know the Book, regardless of whether he or she receives a paycheck from a church or has attended seminary. The accountant should know Numbers as well as she knows numbers. The attorney should know Judges as well as he knows judges. And the politician should know 1 and 2 Kings as well as he knows his favorite legislative kingpins.

As followers of the incarnate Son of God–Son of Man, how could we aim for less? Jesus was "very, very." He was the God-man, very human, very divine. When people try to make Him one or the other, not only do they violate good biblical theology but they end up creating some sort of schizoid Jesus.

The Lord was not "sort of human, very Godlike" or "very human and kind of Godlike." Jesus' spirituality and His humanity were seamless. That is why Jesus could never have been a "great rabbi" but just an "OK carpenter." No, Mark describes Jesus as a *tekton*, a "technician," a master of His craft. Jesus knew how to turn out an excellent product, and He knew how to turn a profit. For Him it was all a part of working as a servant of God in the marketplace. He was "very, very," and so, too, should we be.

Do not think we are denigrating the business leaders who gathered in D.C. We are not. Go to any pastors' conference in the country and survey the clergy and you will likely find the opposite side of the coin. You will find men and women who speak with passion and authority about the Bible, but who hem and haw about the world of work. The world of the church must reacquaint itself with the world of work, for it is here that it has perhaps its largest untapped field of ministry.

We live in a New Economy. Its constantly changing realities have created a heightened sense of insecurity and uncertainty across the entire workforce. The 1980s' comfort blanket of unlimited consumer prosperity is gone. Today people find themselves treading water alone in a global, shark-infested ocean. The twenty-first-century intersection of a cultural hunger and a biblical mandate has created an unprecedented opportunity for ministry. Exploiting it, however, requires the leveraged fulcrum point of God-empowered Life@Work. To be an effective agent of salt and light in this changing chaotic context, a follower of Christ needs to embody a "very, very" mind-set and a "very, very" lifestyle—a person firmly planted in professional excellence and deeply rooted in biblical truth.

The workplace is where the contest over many of today's life issues is being held. When we walk up to the plate, we better have our swing ready. We better be able to hit well *and* run fast. As men and women who long to walk with Christ and to represent Him to the world, we must strive to become "very, very." The church is our dugout, but work is the arena filled with watching, hungry fans where God has called us to play the game.

ONE LAMB ROARING IN A DEN OF LIONS

Bob Briner, our late friend and the longtime president of ProServ Television, came face-to-face with the difficult nature of this task. From humble beginnings, Bob made his way through the ranks of the highly competitive world of professional sports, working in the front office of the Miami Dolphins before launching a career as an agent and then as a television producer. He traveled the world, mingling with some of the wealthiest people on the planet. He was a "player" and he was in the game, but he found himself woefully unprepared to integrate his faith in Jesus with his work.

"As I searched for help in combining Christian living with my world of professional sports and television, it didn't come from my church or denomination," Briner wrote in *Roaring Lambs,* a groundbreaking book challenging believers to impact culture through their work. "And in fairness to this great group of believers, I have not found much help in this area from any of the other traditional evangelical groups."[1]

Briner, who died in 1999 at age sixty-three, set out to become a "very, very" person by infiltrating the cultural citadel of media through his work. As an influential force in the world of professional sports, television, and business, he intentionally, overtly, and skillfully melded the world of Scripture with the world of daily living, and he did it in a profession that is not exactly known for its overwhelming acceptance of believers in Jesus.

His passions included a strong concern that nonbelievers see Jesus in everything we do, especially the skill and excellence of our work. When he met with the shah of Iran, he wanted to evidence Christ. When he negotiated with Akio Morita, the legendary founder of Sony, he wanted to represent Christ. Bob called that being a "Roaring Lamb."

SHEPHERDING ROARING LAMBS

Bob found that his church was as ill-equipped as he was to meet this challenge. While schools and professional associates trained him well to excel in his work, he did not find much training on how to be a follower of Jesus in it—unless he wanted to become a pastor or a missionary. Furthermore, to even take advantage of these biblical training resources, he would have to pack up and move to what he called the "Christian Ghetto." Even the best evangelical seminary education, however, would have little to teach him about what it means to incarnate Christ in the marketplace.

The church, as we currently know it, was simply not designed to equip believers like Charlie and Bob to steward their lives at work. For too long the church has operated as a nursing home and not as a boot camp. In a nursing home, people move in, but they never move out. In a boot camp, you are trained to move out every day, to hit the deck running.

The reason people never move out of the church is that we as a Christian subculture have given up on our culture. We no longer value or prioritize Christian contributions to human endeavor. The church, as Briner noted, "is almost a nonentity when it comes to shaping culture. In the arts, entertainment, media, education, and other culture-shaping venues of our country, the church has abdicated its role as salt and light."[2] The degenerative results of an almost total lack of Christian presence in these arenas are all too tragically obvious.

The winds of change, however, are shifting. It is no longer about Unchurched Harry and Mary; it is about Unconnected, Unfulfilled Charlie. Reaching-and-Empowering Charlie is the transformer for the church of tomorrow. A movement of God is afoot in the workplace. Henry Blackaby has declared, "I've never seen the activity of God this deeply in the business community as I do right now." Billy Graham has similarly said, "I believe one of the next great moves of God is going to be through the believers in the workplace." After thirty years of watching the spiritual weather vane in the corporate world, I would concur. A worldwide spiritual movement is growing in the workplace. It did not start in the church but rather in what the New Testament called the *agora*, the marketplace. It was in the marketplace where life traveled in the first century, and it is in the agora where life intersects today.

There are formal and informal kingdom initiatives popping out in communities all over our country, yes, even all over the world. I believe there are four or five clear indicators that a kingdom movement is afoot. One of the most telling signs is something I call "spiritual entrepreneurship." Although such initiatives vary in size, shape, and color, taken as a whole they demonstrate the Spirit of God actively doing a special work at this time through men and women of faith at work.

Seventeen years ago I participated in a Bible study for men in my hometown. As far as I know, it was the only thing going on at that time anywhere in northwest Arkansas with a bent toward the marketplace.

My, how things have changed. It is staggering to list the specific initiatives in our little community targeting our Life@Work:

- The Summit Business Luncheon
- Work Matters
- Dozens of formal Bible studies
- Untold regular small-group gatherings of men and women who meet weekly at work
- The Influencers Study
- Wal-Mart Vendor Team Leader Friday Morning Bible Study
- Men's Fraternity
- Wild at Heart Weekends
- A Wednesday morning young business professional study
- Campus Crusade business professional efforts
- Probably two dozen different businesses that sponsor a Bible study and prayer time for their employees
- Leadership symposia with a kingdom bent
- Two dozen church-sponsored Bible studies

- AAO Building Champions
- Corporate Chaplains in dozens of different companies
- The Soderquist Center for Business Ethics
- Young Business Leaders from the University of Arkansas Business School
- NorthStar Friday Lunches

These are just the ones I know of. There are probably half as many again with which I am unfamiliar.

Ministry in and to the business community is not new. What is new, however, is the adoption of work-life ministry as a core function of the local church. Christian futurist George Barna has predicted that "workplace ministry will be one of the core future innovations in church ministry."[3] A new ministry paradigm is under development. It is a church that makes work-life discipleship and evangelism part of its stated mission and intentional strategy.

The church of the future must adopt a new structure that targets the Monday-through-Friday side of life, a new strategy helping Charlie Love and Charlie Money get together. The Marketplace Church will focus on where people really traffic, where they really do salt and light. Its pastors will interact regularly with their congregations during the workweek—not just at the hospital bedside, but in the boardroom and on the factory floor.

At the dawn of this realization, many pastors today are making the shift to more effective marketplace ministry. In former days, pastors who preached sermons about work could talk about it only as it related to church committees or offices or service on a church staff. Today pastors are expanding their ministries and messages to be more appropriate to the typical worker out in the world. A paradigm shift is in the works all over the country, even the world. It is a shift from the traditional church program that fostered people's lives at church to a work-life ministry paradigm that fosters their Life@Work. Consider the differences between the two mind-sets:

TRADITIONAL CHURCH PARADIGM

- The organization of the church is the mission.
- Sermons speak in "Churchese" about church categories and topics.
- Bible stories are told through a ministry lens.
- Illustrations are primarily from the pastor's personal world.
- Members are pressured to make church a priority over work.
- Church health is measured in attendance and buildings.
- Everyone is expected to come to the physical location of the church for ministry.
- Spiritual formation is focused on church assimilation.
- Training and mobilization focus on staffing and maintaining the church program.

THE COMING WORK-LIFE CHURCH

- The daily lives of those in the church is the mission.
- Sermons talk in marketplace-friendly language about being salt and light at work.
- Bible characters are painted in all their humanity and daily living.
- Illustrations are from the work-a-day world of the audience.
- Church structure is simplified to free leaders to fulfill their callings.
- Health is measured by the impact of the church's footprint in the community.
- The church initiates training, relationships, and programs out into the marketplace.
- Spiritual formation includes work-life issues of calling, serving, skill, and character development.
- Training and mobilization includes facilitating spiritual entrepreneurship.

The learning curve, however, takes time. Keeping a balanced and integrated life is hard enough without a pastor and church to make the quest harder. Often without even knowing it, a church can cloud the issue—even for churches that are advanced in their appreciation for the workplace!

A SECOND REFORMATION

The Protestant Reformation is widely regarded as one of the most important religious happenings of the second millennium. It traced its roots to Germany, where Johann Gutenberg invented and developed the printing press in the midfifteenth century. The mass printing of Bibles enabled something never before possible: mass biblical literacy. Soon the Bible, once hidden in Latin obscurity, was being studied in the vernacular. Information always effects change. The differences between the current state of the church, its teachings, and Scripture became readily apparent.

These rapid historical developments were driven in part by economics. To raise funds, Pope Leo X had been selling "indulgences." Need to get Cousin Ed out of purgatory? No problem. Worried about your future sins? No problem. Randy Alcorn, in his book *Money, Possessions and Eternity*, points out that when Johann Tetzel came to town "selling forgiveness as if it were a sack of potatoes or a pair of shoes"[4] on behalf of the pope, a local priest became fed up with the system. That priest was Martin Luther. In 1517 Luther nailed his ninety-five theses calling for reform to the door of the church in Wittenberg.

The Reformation had begun. Luther, John Calvin, and others provided the message, and Gutenberg provided the means to distribute it. The world would never be the same.

The Reformation was a significant factor in all of the developments that followed: the progress made in science, in medicine, in education, in theology, in the arts, and the development of democracy. These changes became reality largely because of the insatiable interest in Scripture. Thanks to Gutenberg's printing press, the Bible finally became accessible to the common person. The average person could read and understand it; that change became the catalyst for life coming together in ways almost incomprehensible to us today.

Think about it. People were living in the "dark ages" of civilization. They lived in ignorance, with little or no authority, freedom, autonomy, or permission to develop a personal relationship with Jesus Christ based on the content of His revelation in Scripture. Then someone put Bibles in their hands and said, "See for yourselves!" The Bible became the tool that all people of all nations at all times could hold in their hands and say, "This has connection to my world."

People searched for God. Culture—all of humanity—reaped the benefits. I am sorry to disappoint today's New Agers and Eastern spiritualists, but such dramatic change did not happen in the seventh century when people worshipped crystals; it happened when truth began to permeate all areas of life. When God's truth and life are not confined to a box, then big things happen; the world changes beyond human explanation.

Although creativity, innovation, and discovery remain a part of our world, in many arenas, man has put God back in his box. People seem determined to go it alone, to use only human intellect and skill while plumbing the house, selling the toys, managing the project team, operating on the sick, sculpting the statue, researching the cure for disease, or drafting the design for an office building. But when we include God—when we live a "very, very" life—the big becomes bigger, the great becomes greater, the impossible becomes possible.

A second reformation can herald the same dramatic change.

Again, we see an insatiable interest in Scripture, but this time with an eye toward its application in our professional work life, a frontier where biblical knowledge and influence have been seriously lacking. What is new is not the *availability* of Scripture to the common citizen, but the *application* of Scripture to the common life—all areas of it. We have a new opportunity to bring God out of the box (as if mortals could keep Him there!) and experience His wonders at work in the marketplace.

It is none too soon, for as British essayist Dorothy Sayers lamented, "In nothing has the church so lost her hold on reality as in her failure to understand and respect the secular vocation, she has allowed work and religion to become separate departments . . . She has forgotten that the secular vocation is sacred." And if the church no longer sees work as sacred, is it any wonder that so many workers no longer see their faith as sacred? "How can anyone remain interested in a religion," asked Sayers, "that seems to have no concern with nine-tenths of life?"

There are many other Charlies out there today who have yet to encounter the radical life-changing power of Christ. It is for their sake that we, as individuals and as the body of Christ, must recommit ourselves to a new reformation effort to reexplain the relevance of God to daily life. It is no longer acceptable to leave on our nightstands the Bibles that were brought to us thanks to Gutenberg and Luther. We must walk into the office with the Word written across our work lives. We must reintegrate our faith and our career.

The church, however, must be restructured to intentionally and systematically nurture these needed changes. Ultimately, there will be no lasting changes to our Life@Work until there are lasting changes to our Church@Work. If we do not change the church from within, someone will one day be nailing the notice of our deficiencies to our doors as well.

Whatever we do, we can know this for sure: our enemy already has an active marketplace ministry, right here in my town, targeting the work lives of my neighbors with his systematic plan of death and devastation. Like David, our nation is being ravaged by a Goliath pillaging work lives every day. Who will stand to oppose him? Who will dare take what stones they have, walk out into the battlefield, and reclaim it in the name of the Lord? Where will we draw the line? If not our places of work, then where? If not my church, who? If not now, when?

In many ways our Life@Work is the most distinguishing signature any of us scribble into our legacies. We all will leave our mark. Don't travel the journey without the four quiet but powerful weapons of calling, serving, character, and skill. The expedition is too demanding, and the stakes are too high. Truly, when people of faith and churches of vision activate calling, character, skill, and serving, the workplace will spark a spiritual transformation unlike anything seen by those alive today. Get serious about your Life@Work.

Notes

1. Darrel Collins, quoted in Donald Patterson, "First in Flight: Countdown to Takeoff," *News & Record*, 8-22-99, www.news-record.com.

1. George Orwell, *Animal Farm* (New York: Signet Classic, 1996), 133. Full Quote: "All animals are equal but some are more equal than others."
2. William Barclay, *The Mind of Jesus* (New York: Harper & Row, 1960), 9.

1. Marcus Buckingham and Donald O. Clifton, *Now, Discover Your Strengths* (New York: Free Press, 2001), 6.
2. Ibid., 19.

1. Os Guinness, *The Call* (Nashville, Word Publishing, 1998). 29.

1. M. Easton, *Easton's Bible Dictionary* (1996, c1897).
2. http://www.quotationspage.com/quotes/W._Somerset_Maugham/.

1. Jim Collins, *Good to Great* (New York: Harper Collins, 2001).
2. Richard Bolles, *What Color Is Your Parachute?* (Berkeley, CA: Ten Speed Press, 2001).
3. Henry Blackaby, *Experiencing God* (Nashville: Broadman & Holman Publishers, 1994).

1. C. S. Lewis, *The Collected Works of C. S. Lewis* (Inspirational, 1996), 223.
2. Stephen R. Graves and Thomas G. Addington, *The Fourth Frontier* (Nashville: Word Publishing, 2000), 32.

1. Edythe Draper, *Draper's Book of Quotations for the Christian World* (Wheaton, Ill.: Tyndale House Publishers, Inc., 1992), 555.

2. Robert K. Greenleaf, *On Becoming a Servant-Leader*, ed. Don M. Frick and Larry C. Spears (New York: Paulist Press, 1977), 31.

CHAPTER 13
1. Belle Linda Halpern and Kathy Lubar, *Leadership Presence* (New York: Gotham, 2003).

CHAPTER 14
1. Oswald Sanders, *Bible Men of Faith* (Chicago: Moody, 1965), 123.
2. Ibid., 121.
3. Del Jones, "Was the Writing on the Wall, . . . or on Their Annual Reports?" *USA Today*, 29 March 2004, 3B.

CHAPTER 15
1. Charles Swindoll, *Paul, A Man of Grit and Grace* (Nashville: W Publishing, 2002), 65.
2. Robert Browning, "Understanding Suffering,"
3. George Patton, *Patton's Principles*.

CHAPTER 16
1. John Maxwell with Stephen Graves and Thomas Addington, *The Power of One* (Nashville: Thomas Nelson, 2004).

CONCLUSION
1. Bob Briner, *Roaring Lambs* (Grand Rapids: Zondervan, 1993), 15.
2. Ibid., 28.
3. George Barna and Mark Hatch, *Boiling Point* (Ventura, CA: Regal Publishing, 2003).
4. Randy Alcorn, *Money, Possessions and Eternity* (Wheaton: Tyndale, 1989).

Some information not specifically endnoted was found on the following four Web sites:

www.creativequotations.com
www.famousquotes.com
www.quotationpage.com
www.psalm121.ca

About the Authors

JOHN C. MAXWELL, known as America's expert on leadership, speaks in person to hundreds of thousands of people each year. He has communicated his principles to Fortune 500 companies, the United States Military Academy at West Point, international marketing organizations, the NCAA, and professional sports groups such as the NFL. Maxwell is the founder of several leadership organizations, including Maximum Impact, helping people reach their personal and leadership potential. A *New York Times* bestselling author, Dr. Maxwell has written more than thirty books, including *Developing the Leader Within You, Thinking for a Change, There's No Such Thing as Business Ethics,* and *The 21 Irrefutable Laws of Leadership,* which has sold more than one million copies.

STEPHEN R. GRAVES and THOMAS G. ADDINGTON have been business partners and best friends for almost two decades. For the last fifteen years, they have been exploring how to blend business excellence with biblical wisdom through consulting, teaching, mentoring, and writing. This mission statement, originally scratched out on a breakfast napkin early one morning twelve years ago, has been their "never lost" system as they have journeyed through a variety of entrepreneurial endeavors and experiments.

They founded Cornerstone Consulting Group and the *Life@Work Journal;* they speak regularly in business, ministry, and academic settings; they publish frequently; they serve on national boards; and they are active in coaching leaders toward the finish line. Both hold earned doctorates, both are deeply devoted to their families, and both love the never-ending challenge of meshing real life with the message of Jesus. They have authored fifteen books or booklets.

Life@Work
Companion Workbook

The *Life@Work* Companion Workbook will help you build on what you have already learned from the *Life@Work* book. Go deeper into this practical study by dissecting, analyzing, and then implementing each and every principle into your everyday work life. The lesson text brings focus to maintaining your balance with your faith and work, and the in-depth study questions assist in giving you a deeper understanding of how you can effectively merge your faith with the rest of your life. To ensure you take measurable steps toward improvement, application suggestions are provided with this study to help you create your own action points.

Let us help you live your life of faith to the fullest — pre-order your copy of the *Life@Work* Companion Workbook today at **www.lifeatwork.com**!

Introducing the Complete Life@Work Ministry Program!

Let the *Life@Work* Program help you generate enormous buzz and goodwill in your community! By hosting a simulcast once a year for the business professionals in your area, your church will have the foundation in place to provide a **powerful outreach program** aimed at merging faith into the workplace to impact your neighborhood.

Launching a ministry of this caliber for this audience has been a daunting task in the past — mainly because very few resources exist that have real meaning to busy business professionals. Current work resources that are available rarely hit home for participants and poorly relate to real business issues. Solving this problem has been the mission for *Life@Work* and we believe the *Life@Work* **Program is the definitive answer.**

Your church ministry or small group can pick and choose what portions of the program best fit their mission as well. The *Life@Work* Program includes: **The *Life@Work* Groupzine series, *Life@Work* resources, *Life@Work* Simulcast, *Life@Work* Symposium,** and additional modules and training will be available over time. Select the programs that best fit your needs and finances and begin building your workplace ministry outreach today!

Life@Work
Groupzine Series

Small groups are the core of many successful ministries. A *Life@Work* **Workplace ministry** is designed to work in the same fashion as a small group. *Life@Work* offers small groups for singles, couples, women, thirty-somethings, just to name a few. To assist these groups we offer the *Life@Work* **Groupzine Series.** These groupzines are a new and innovative approach to theme-based curriculum study. We combine the best elements of a magazine and small group study into one effective resource that can service the individual and the small group.

Life@Work Groupzines aid and assist workplace leaders to engage in topics relevant to their members' professional and personal lives. This interaction leads to powerful discussions and spiritual renewal. Covered areas in the groupzines  include issues that workplace professionals face on an ongoing basis, including: balance, calling, ambition, stewardship, power, and skill. Implement ongoing life change through small group settings in your church, office or at the local Starbucks!

This powerful study will make a significant impact on the lives of the business professionals in your community. Learn more on these small group studies by visiting **www.lifeatwork.com.**

Life@Work
Resources

To make a continued, reverberating impact in the marketplace, we need faith-friendly resources that add immense value to a business professional. *Life@Work* resources include various training programs by best-selling author John C. Maxwell. *Learning the 21 Irrefutable Laws of Leadership, Winning With People,* and *Learning the 17 Indisputable Laws of Teamwork* DVD training courses are excellent programs your workplace ministry can host that can attract additional businesspeople.

This training also adds value to your church's current crop of business leaders — allowing them to see that your church has their needs and personal growth in mind.

Additional resources are planned and being developed that will help provide continual training for a workplace ministry leader and those who take part in the training.

Please visit **www.lifeatwork.com** for additional information and updates on upcoming resource and training releases.

Life@Work
Simulcast

There is no better way to make an instant, powerful impact among the business professionals in your community than with a proven leadership training event featuring some of the greatest business minds and leaders of our time. Previous speakers at this event have included: **John Wooden, Pat Summitt, Lou**  **Holtz, Joe Gibbs, Ken Blanchard, Brian Tracy, Zig Ziglar,** and **John C. Maxwell.** Broadcast in over 500 churches each year, this LIVE training event is the ideal catalyst to launch your workplace ministry.

Dispel the notion that your church is out of touch with 21st century professionals and draw in the business leaders in your community. This event will define your church as **the church** in your area **known for taking care of business.**

Life@Work Symposium

The most crucial aspect of any ministry is the struggle to maintain a relevant edge amongst its participants. Picture a current singles group using material and teaching styles from 1970 (scary, isn't it?). Remaining current allows a ministry to continually grow. Even more so, a workplace ministry must remain relevant. Business professionals won't sacrifice the time unless the material "delivers the goods." To remain on the forefront, *Life@Work* created the ***Life@Work* Symposium**. This gathering includes pastors, key workplace ministry leaders, business professionals, and noted experts to provide training for workplace ministry leaders and generate up-to-date, relevant content and study materials for the business professional.

Symposium participants will walk away from this event equipped and encouraged with resources and follow-up strategies for reaching their laity as well as the business community. Workplace ministry leaders are given a strategic plan to teach to and connect with the members of the study. Consider this Symposium experience a crash course in "*Wall Street Journal* meets Scripture."

Learn more about the ***Life@Work* Symposium** at **www.lifeatwork.com**.